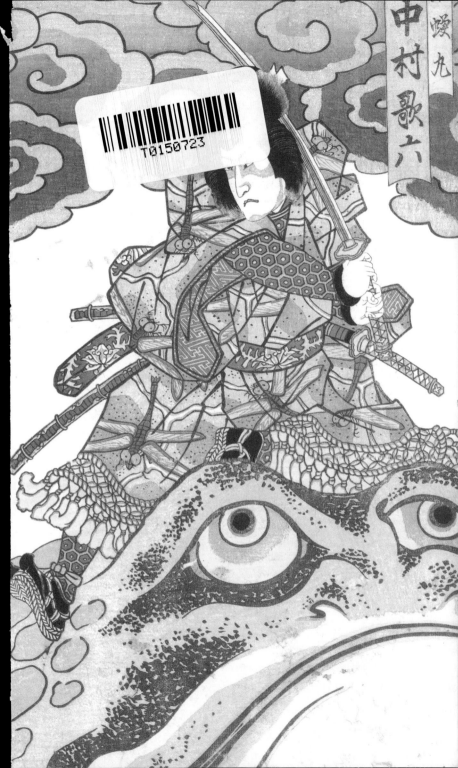

THE ART
OF LIFE
AND DEATH

THE ART
OF LIFE
AND DEATH

Lessons in Budo from a Ninja Master

foreword by **Masaaki Hatsumi**

SLEIMAN AZIZI *and* **DANIEL FLETCHER**

TUTTLE Publishing

Tokyo | Rutland, Vermont | Singapore

Published by Tuttle Publishing, an imprint of Periplus Editions (HK) Ltd.

www.tuttlepublishing.com

Copyright © 2012 Sleiman Azizi and Daniel Fletcher

Library of Congress Cataloging-in-Publication Data

Azizi, Sleiman.
  The art of life and death : lessons in budo from a ninja master / Sleiman Azizi and Daniel Fletcher ; [foreword by] Masaaki Hatsumi.
    p. cm.
   ISBN 978-0-8048-4304-1 (hardback)
  1. Martial arts--Japan--Philosophy. 2. Bushido. I. Fletcher, Daniel. II. Title.
  GV1100.77.A2A95 2012
  796.8150952--dc23

                        2012001806

ISBN 978-0-8048-4304-1

Distributed by
North America, Latin America &
Europe

Tuttle Publishing
364 Innovation Drive
North Clarendon, VT 05759-9436
U.S.A.
Tel: 1 (802) 773-8930
Fax: 1 (802) 773-6993
info@tuttlepublishing.com
www.tuttlepublishing.com

Japan
Tuttle Publishing
Yaekari Building, 3rd Floor
5-4-12 Osaki,
Shinagawa-ku, Tokyo 141 0032
Tel: (81) 3 5437-0171
Fax: (81) 3 5437-0755
tuttle-sales@gol.com

Asia Pacific
Berkeley Books Pte. Ltd.
61 Tai Seng Avenue #02-12
Singapore 534167
Tel: (65) 6280-1330
Fax: (65) 6280-6290
inquiries@periplus.com.sg
www.periplus.com

First edition
12 11 10 09 08
10 9 8 7 6 5 4 3 2 1   1207RP

Printed in China

TUTTLE PUBLISHING® is a registered trademark of Tuttle Publishing, a division of Periplus Editions (HK) Ltd.

*This book is dedicated to our fallen **buyu**:*

Abi Allen
Kathy Baylor
Mark Hodel
Dick Severance
Greg Dilley
Nich Ermak
Butch Johnson
Jaco Zwanepoel
Glenn Morris

And to all of the victims of the Tohoku earthquake
of March, 2011.
May God have mercy on their souls.

Contents

Foreword

I have been asked to write a few words by way of a foreword for this newly published book by Sleiman Azizi and Daniel Fletcher.

At the moment, there are thousands upon thousands of Bujinkan students throughout the world. Naturally, the evidence of the martial efforts of some of these students is reflected in the books and DVDs that they themselves publish. And of course, I have a look at each of these works every time one is released. I am delighted that some of them have been able to grow and mature enough to be able to do so.

With this in mind, it is a great pleasure for me to be able to see the evidence of Sleiman and Daniel's own efforts in the martial arts through the publication of this book. I consider this book to be an important one for any person who wishes to understand budo.

Congratulations to the both of you on the publication of this book and good luck to you with the writing of your next one!

Masaaki Hatsumi
Bujinkan Dojo Soke

Introduction

Who would visit a museum where every painting and sculpture was made from the blood and bones of people who had been killed?

It is a macabre thought but, believe it or not, it does exist. Regardless of how you feel about the morality of such a thing, it is real. Budo is a living, human museum. Each and every exhibit was crafted from the agony and death of a human being. Despite the awful suffering that bore it, and possibly because of it, we have a duty as moral people to learn everything that such a costly collection can teach us. This has nothing to do with fighting: It is ancient, concentrated truth. It is also pure art. All true art is borne of human suffering. No matter who or what you are, these priceless teachings will change your deepest self.

Infinitely more than just punching and kicking, the martial arts are about death. (And life for those who survive.) In this day and age, the somber issues of life and death are often considered the sole province of the military and police, but for most of human history, war was a quotidian fact. Men, women and children were intimately familiar with the sights, sounds, and smells of death. However, the budo that was born from this visceral reality has quietly slipped into obscurity. What we call "martial arts" has now become a form of athletic competition. Warfare and the struggle for survival have become branches of science and engineering. It is very hard for the average person to connect modern martial arts with their ghastly origins.

Despite the modern illusion of peace, the life and death struggle continues. Surprisingly, martial artists who understand this still exist. As students of the old budo, we should have been prepared for this reality, but we were not. Many surprises awaited us when we came to Japan. One was that the notions we brought with us to Japan about budo were totally incorrect.

Just as our teacher had said, we discovered that budo was not about forms and that it was not about being strong or weak. Nor was it about being skilled or unskilled. And again, just as our teacher said, we learned that art was the life of the budoka.

"Many of the things I teach you are beautiful.
They are also terrible, awful things.
You need both to survive."

Some people understand this, yet many more do not. We wondered why. It is not that students of the martial arts are intentionally studying or practicing the wrong way; they are innocent. Nor is it necessarily true that their instructors are intentionally teaching them "bad budo." The challenge facing us is the fact that many of the most important concepts in budo are emotionally draining, requiring a totally honest self-analysis and a willingness to admit to, and purge, our own faults.

It is no wonder that a person might have trouble understanding when he may only hear such troubling words once a year in a foreign language that may or may not be clearly translated. The temptation to disregard what doesn't make sense is strong, particularly if you find it anathema to what you thought you knew about budo. For some, these teachings will produce an intensely negative reaction; for others, it will spark the beginnings of Satori (Enlightenment).

This is something that needs to be illuminated clearly: Our opinions on budo come straight from the grandmaster himself, not just from reading his books or watching his videos (which we also do). We listened to him speak, in person, every week, for a combined total of more than 17 years. Whenever there was something we didn't understand, we went directly to him and asked him, accepting whatever it was he said (even though we didn't understand). So many questions about so many subjects! He was, and still is, always patient, open and direct with his answers.

Irrespective Of

These things exist
Even if you cannot see them
And they are waiting
Even if you are not.

There are no secrets in budo, there are only lessons we refuse to learn.

Our intention in writing this book has been to share some of our discoveries as a form of gratitude to our teacher. What we are presenting are lessons learned by listening to the grandmaster. They were also learned by not listening to him and learning things the hard way, by trial and costly error.

There is a Japanese proverb that admonishes the student not to step on the shadow of his teacher. In writing this book, we discovered that no matter how hard you try to avoid stepping on it, your teacher's shadow will always cover you. So, while this book comes from our own personal discoveries, we hope that more than anything, it will be seen as a testament to the vitality of the grandmaster and his budo.

"Budo is art and it is connected to all other arts.
Even in the midst of battle, art can be found.
At least, for those who survive."

This book may seem to be about fighting: it is not. This book is about the essence of art and the essence of the artist, whether jazz musician or sculptor.

Budo is art. It must be seen as art and not as information that you "know." How important do you feel it is to "possess information" like the names of techniques, the "proper angles" of the feet, etc…? How important is it for you to move "correctly?" After all, movement is also a kind of information. To believe that knowing such things is important is not such a terrible thing, but it would be misleading to call it art, let alone budo.

"Budo is art. We are bu-geisha, not budo-ka."
(Artists whose medium is war as
opposed to students of fighting)

"More than being a budoka,
we are bugeika.
We are artists."

Art is a mystery. It is also never-ending creation. Thinking that you understand creativity because you have looked at many paintings is to put the cart before the horse. Our goal is not to become "art experts," but "painters." Perhaps this is something that can only be understood after the fact. Budo is not something that can be seen; only the end result is visible. And yet, for many, watching a demonstration of real budo results only in an incredulous, "Is that all there is?"

In the world of budo, yes, that is all.

"It takes a certain kind of vision to know that something is art. What's more, this vision has less to do with the eyes and more to do with the heart. How important this heart is! There are many who will tell you of the importance of knowing things. Many of them are even good people, but they are not artists."

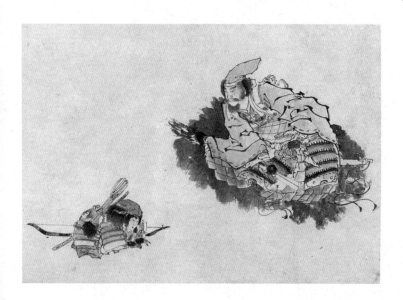

Caveat Emptor

"Don't teach people stuff they don't need.
This is dangerous stuff; it is only need-to-know."

We are martial artists; we have nothing to show for all of our hard work and years of study. If we did, we wouldn't be martial artists. We would speak to your senses then, and hope that your senses can convince you of something more, something greater.

Budo is a mystery. Beyond any boundaries of language and geography, its lessons flow, touching the hearts of all who listen. Some people limit their willingness to listen beyond a certain point. Budo crosses that, too. On the edges of comprehension, these lessons live in the hearts of the patient. Budo can be very difficult to understand. Budo is truly a mystery.

Budo is a beast. Budo may resonate within the heart but it will also tear it apart. The roster of the dead is a long one. The ones who survive physically must contend with a living carcass, with a spirit drained by the knowing of humanity's darkest secrets. Budo can be very hard to accept. The beast is always hungry, and budo's fangs are long. Budo will teach you things you do not like.

Budo is powerful. Poetic as all of this seems, it is not fantasy. For those who are new to budo, this is a real warning: Touching the heart of human suffering is traumatic. For those who have experienced the agony of throwing the self away, hopefully you will find comfort in knowing that you are not alone. If the healing process is not yet complete, you may find that this book tears open wounds even deeper than before. Budo will overwhelm you.

Budo is costly. To study budo is to study change. To understand change, you yourself must be changed. There is a price you must pay to understand. Budo gives with one hand and takes with the other. It is one thing to know that budo doesn't come cheap, but it is quite another to actually pay with a piece of your soul. In budo, unlike in most exchanges, when you pay you get nothing tangible in return. In a very real sense, you are paying to throw your self away. Budo can be very hard to bear.

Budo becomes you. There will come a day when you no longer recognize your own face in the mirror and you can never get it back. For a time, the price of this change will weigh on you heavily. Some never recover and spend their time trying to relive how things were before. Others live with the bitterness of not being able to come to terms with "being right." If you can persevere with the demons in the teachings, you will come to see the angels as well. Yes, you will be a different person.

Between now and then, however:
You will feel woefully inadequate.
You will feel physically ill.
You will be shocked.
You will lose friends.
You will have nightmares.

Now that you know the severity of the cost, you should show budo the respect that it deserves when you make your decision. Nobody exhumes a body without a damn good reason and if they must, they do everything humanly possible to learn as much as they can from what they find. The very least we owe the dead is sincere respect. (When you train, this is what you do—you speak with the dead.)

Remember also that you have a choice. There is no shame in turning away. If you don't need budo, then you should not study it. Budo can break your heart and nobody should have to suffer that without a good reason. If you do make the choice, then be joyful with the knowledge that you will come to know a freedom unlike any other.

The flowers that grow on Mount St. Helens are the most beautiful on Earth. I don't envy them their beauty. I envy their courage.

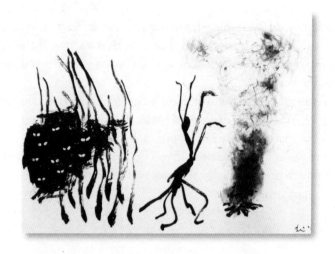

The Three Paths to Nowhere

Bloodlines drawn, we saved ourselves
Never counting the cost.
Yet having paid, the time has come
To let it all go.

You have to wonder if old people drive so slowly because they can't see well anymore or because they have seen too much.

Wargames

Little boy soldier
Did you forget
That you can
Never go home?

Danger Signs

Beware the written word,
And the spoken thought.

Moon Shine

You, who have not
Seen the falling moon,
Perhaps it is you
I should envy.

"He jests at scars that never felt a wound."
—William Shakespeare

Dragon's Breath

Someone disappeared
For you to come forth.
This is the way of it,
  The dark place.

Someone's was shed
For yours to flow.
This is the cost of it,
  The dark place.

Someone stared into nothing
For you to forget
Though they remember it,
  The dark place.

But there are some
Who breathe fire
Lighting the way,
Out of the dark place.

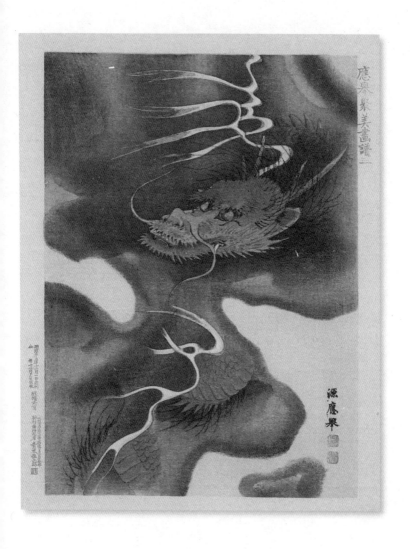

Nature

"If it isn't natural, it isn't right."

Every year, between 5,000 and 10,000 people are killed by animals worldwide. (It is estimated that about 30% of them are also eaten by those animals.) It is possible that those numbers are understated by 50%. A small percentage of those deaths are accidental, a few more are "mistakes," but the remaining thousands are intentional killings. Most are predation (for food), but many are just killings. Every animal kills. Even the animals we think of as "cute" may be savage killers in their own way. This does not make them "bad." It is the natural way of survival for all things. Nature is not kind. Nature is not fair. The power of nature dwarfs anything man can achieve.

Above all these things though, budo is natural. It is important to study nature closely. Nature and what is natural are often equated with elegance and poise, an effortlessness that stems from control and discipline. But this is to confuse human constructs with what actually exists "out there." Nature can be very violent, rough, coarse, and in many cases, ruthless. It can also be warm, beautiful and breathtakingly peaceful. There is a profound beauty in this seemingly contradictory aspect of nature. Make no mistake about it; human beauty is a wonderful thing. But is it wrong to suggest that natural beauty is even greater? Every artist who has ever lived has envied "God's abilities with the brush."

> *"An artist, under pain of oblivion, must have confidence in himself, and listen only to his real master: Nature."* —Renoir

Whatever it is, it always happens as it happens. Our thoughts, desires, concerns, and hopes can also be seen as natural. They too, occur. And yet, these naturally occurring emotions and impulses are the very same things that hold us back in our understanding of nature in budo and of budo in nature. Nature does not follow our rules and limitations. This is so important that it bears repeating: Nature does not follow our rules and limitations. Only we are bound by our rules and limitations. In nature, changes happen when changes happen and we have no say in the matter.

Like Canadian geese migrating south for the winter, you either move freely with natural changes or you die.

Learning budo in most dojos is like learning about animals in a zoo. You can watch them from a safe distance, study their habits and learn every academic thing about them. That is not the same as understanding nature. You are probably not actually in danger of being killed nor do you even feel any such fear. That is not natural. If you really wanted to understand nature, you'd have to spend a few months in the woods with the grizzly bears sniffing around your tent every night. If you survive, you may not find the zoo so charming anymore.

Real nature will tear you to pieces and eat you without warning or regret. So it is with real budo.

The monolith scene from *2001: A Space Odyssey* often comes into my mind. I wonder, "What exactly did the monolith expect the monkeys to do?" Watching them smash bones into the dirt and on each other seems like such a vulgar, violent, ignorant sort of response. But my judgments are human judgments and do not apply to nature. They DO seem to enjoy it.

Movement

Silence, in seeing
Stillness, in motion
Sound, resonating
For a time until,
Recollection.

There is a doorway at the bottom of a hill. There is no door, but it is dark inside, so most people do not enter. Animals often go inside to seek shelter from the snow: squirrels and skunks and porcupines. They see a door and they go through, a perfectly natural thing to do.

"Nature is infinite; both nothing and everything.
In this way, it has unfathomable power."

Change

Of itself, occurring,
Not caused, but accepting,
Change is breath, life living
Its breath, blood giving
Between one and the next.

The softest, sweetest fruit is the peach. Anyone can eat the peach. Her skin is soft and her flesh is soft and yields easily to the teeth and the lips. A baby can eat a peach. Even her color is easy on the eyes. But the heart of the peach—the part you can't see? Hard as a rock and full of poison.

A poetic man once wrote a poem about a tiger. He admired the beast for its form, its color, its grace. The poetic man did not hear the woman scream and gurgle as she died, he did not feel her dragged from her bed, he did not hear bones crunching, did not piss himself with fear, he did not smell the blood, he did not see the pitiful remains. The tiger is a beautiful animal.

What will you do when the Earthquake hits? Are you ready? Can you stop it from happening? Are you strong, ready and able? Show me how you will do it.

"No matter how strong you are, a natural disaster will defeat you." (February 20th, 2011)

There was a professional African big-game hunter who, after he retired, said that every time he went to the movies and the MGM Lion roared on the big screen, it filled him with fear.

The men and women of the sea know the truth. Surfers, sailors, and fishermen know. You ride the waves and ride the wind and maybe you come home alive. You cannot challenge the wind and waves and if you try, you will never be seen again.

It is said that if a bug could hang on to a horse's tail, he could ride a thousand miles. Indeed, it may even be a simple thing to do. But at the end of the ride, the bug will stink of horseshit and be a very long way from home.

Any animal, by letting nature take its course, can make a life: A perfect, new life. Frankenstein, with all his intelligence and science, his parts and pieces sewn together, could only make a monster: A miserable creature.

Mother Nature

Let them make their stand.
It makes no difference,
To Her.

Change

"Budo is change. This is important."

If someone were to define budo, they would more than likely use the word "change" in their definition. Without change, there would be no life and without life, there would be no budo. If the student of budo learns nothing else but this, they will have learned a lot. Without change, budo cannot be. Change is the lifeblood of budo and of the budoka.

It is perfectly natural to grab on to that which is most precious to us, but even that will leave us when our time comes. Change, budo's most important principle, can be seen in every facet of life.

"Kimattenai!" (Nothing is decided.)

Change can be seen consciously but the change itself is not a conscious phenomenon. It exists at all levels, and occurs, as it will. You may discover laws describing that change but at some further level, those laws and descriptions cease to be effective. There is no starting point for it nor is there an end point. This expression of change is continuous. It never stops. If the budoka has a talent, it would be his or her capacity to recognize change. If he or she has a defining characteristic, it would be that their lives are lived adapting to such changes. This way of living is unremarkable to an outside observer, the changes being imperceptible.

> *"Have no beginning and no end."*

Change is a survival strategy, and naturally so. All life, no matter what merit we attach to it, will disappear if it cannot change. Conditions may nurture complacency in one while options drown another. There are no guarantees when it comes to survival. The word "change" in English has many meanings, but the sense of change in budo is one of an endless series of very temporary, often imperceptible changes; Changes in attitude, position, color, mood. The world—and the opponent—is changing constantly and we must change with them or perish.

> *"Art is never finished, only abandoned."*
> —Leonardo DaVinci

Of course, this is not a new concept; the theory of adaptation and natural selection has been around for many decades. Budo requires us to change and adapt to changes nanosecond by nanosecond without resistance. It is difficult to remove one's resistance to that change but it is possible. That possibility reminds us that one does not "add" budo to one's self. One is changed by budo. You will be changed into one who changes readily.

> *"Don't ever think to yourself*
> *"Now I'll use my budo!"*
> *Just keep changing with him, control yourself and*
> *maintain your connection."*

In the actual nuts and bolts of training practice, one begins by moving the body, adjusting endlessly as the opponent dictates.

Your mind can change and become more flexible but that doesn't mean that you understand budo. Many are skilled at techniques but do not go beyond this level of understanding. If your spirit changes so that your totality is capable of endless, spontaneous change, then you will have understood.

When you are "doing budo," there is absolutely no telling where you will end up. This is budo in action. Following predetermined forms is a death-trap. A more subtle trap is the desire to use what you know while waiting for the opponent to change.

Your ability to change instantly is something the opponent will not be able to understand and his will to fight will be sapped by this. There are an infinite number of moments in a fight where nothing physical is actually happening. In those empty moments you can change yourself. It need not be a total transformation; just a little movement may be sufficient, but you have to be aware of the proper time to change and seeing its effect, be ready to change yet again.

Masters always appear to be in the perfect place. They always appear to be doing the perfect move every time. But in truth, there is no perfection going on. Just change. There is no planning to be in the right place. Just change. There is no plan to set up the opponent. Just change. In a very real sense, the opponent is creating the circumstances and the master is changing with him over and over until the opponent kills himself. In budo, he who is no longer able to change dies first.

"You must be able to play, to change constantly."

Surviving budo is a challenge. The weight of its understanding can be heavy. If you try to hold on to that understanding, the changes around you will pass you by and you will be left behind. A light heart, freed from the restrictions of knowing has a wonderfully natural ability to float from one moment to the next. Circumstances may be severe but the budoka can live between them, playfully changing all the while.

Spinner

The pinwheel knows!
He ends up, every time,
In the right spot.

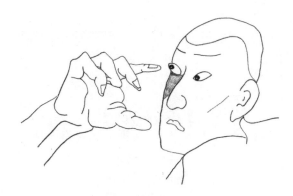

Every time you dance the tango, your feet land in a different place, and yet, it's still the tango. How can this be?

*"If you cannot change,
then you cannot do budo."*

The best jazz musicians can't even play a simple song all the way through.

There were two fools who followed a straight road. They claimed to be explorers.

There was a man who used to carry an umbrella opened above his head. Inside or outside, rain or shine, his umbrella was always open. When asked why he carried an open umbrella everywhere he went, the man replied, "The weather never changes when I carry this umbrella."

"Don't do anything until you pick up the signal."

Directives

*We see steps
Towards a place
Where none step
But to their end.*

How unpredictable a newborn child's movement is! Is this a sign of madness, or of development?

Have you ever wondered at how a mosquito is always *not* where you expect it to be? It's maddening when trying to catch one.

Beginnings

The seasons change,
Time to die.

Patience

*"If you can't wait until the very last moment,
you will die."*

It is very easy to conjure up images of feline stealth or the spiritual wisdom of an ancient master when considering patience in the martial arts. One can also reasonably imagine patience as being related to a life of steadfast discipline and commitment. With patience, as with every part of budo, there is something more, something much deeper.

Expectations are difficult to throw away. When you discard your expectations of what you think budo is, patience begins its work. To be able to wait, knowing that you do not know what will happen, knowing that something could go wrong, is terrifying. In budo, as in life, you don't go about your business with a secret pride in knowing the future. You live your life with nonchalant buoyancy. This is natural and proper.

One has to let go of everything and ride whatever waves come along. It is hard to ride waves when you are forever grabbing onto imagined handholds. These handholds expertly hide themselves within our ideas, beliefs and expectations. To be able to recognize them requires honest skills of observation. You must rid yourself of handholds; they don't keep you up, they hold you down. The ninja were famous as spies but once the battle was over, one had to be able to observe the damage to one's self. Such observation skills are of prime importance in budo.

> *"Adopt the pace of nature: her secret is patience."*
> —R.W. Emerson

To be able to wait for the opponent is the basis of movement in budo. One doesn't wait for the opponent to move simply because one is waiting to get him. One waits because waiting allows you to survive. When the opponent moves, (and people can move internally as well as externally) his intention moves you. If you do not wait for his intention to move you, you may or may not avoid his attack.

The words "ninja" and "shinobi" represent fantastic images to many people but both words are formed from the same kanji character meaning "to wait," "to put up with" and "to endure." There is a reason for this. A ninja, therefore, can be said to be someone who waits—a patient person. When you think you should move, don't. Wait to see what happens. Let what happens guide you. How many people would associate patience with life-or-death combat? Not many. And yet, budo truly is about waiting. You must be patient and show self-restraint.

"Do only what is absolutely necessary to be safe and then wait until things change and it becomes necessary to do something else."

One might construe this as meaning that one should be passive and forgiving; that is not necessarily the case, at least, not when someone is trying to kill you. What it means is that we have to wait for that moment, that window of opportunity, wherein the opponent has set his mind on a path of action and he is no longer fully aware of you. No matter his strength, in that moment, he is weak. He may be stabbing with a knife, and that is a dangerous state of affairs, but his mind is in the knife, his mind is in his stabbing movement. During that window, you can change yourself in some way and what he thought was inevitable ceases to be. He will become confused and try to regain his awareness of what is around him. If you can wait for this moment to arrive (no matter how long it takes), you can survive, but you have to be patient.

"You are waiting for his reaction."

In the beginning, it is natural to focus only on physical movement but many people never move on from there and their patience, such as it is, remains skill-centered. The more you wait, the more you let happen naturally and the more you will know what will happen next. This is not a conscious observation but a full-body one. In budo, this is known as *ishiki o nobasu*, an extension or development of one's awareness. Your body will know to move. You will feel what is dangerous to you. Patience allows this ability to arise. Patience allows you to see what is around you. Without patience, all you will see is yourself. Any hard and fast, kick-and-punch ideas about budo preclude this ability.

"You need to be able to sense with everything,
all the way down to your toes."

It takes tremendous courage to wait. It takes guts and heart to just "be there," sensing the world around you with every inch of your skin and allowing yourself to have no plans for victory, but that is exactly what you have to do.

"Don't feel like you need to do anything; just wait
for the opponent to make up his mind."

Expectations

This, the silent terror
Waiting on the edges
Of knowing.
"Don't worry about what comes next."

Patterns in the Night

I see visions, a swirling darkness
Filled with empty moments.
Light moves and I wonder
I do wonder, what it all means.

There once was a comedian who brought the audience to its feet with applause. He only stood there on the stage, without moving or speaking, until the very last moment. Andy Kaufman understood.

Giant Strides

The secret of the patient man?
No one can see him move.

"If you have to ask what jazz is, you'll never know!"
—Louis Armstrong

In order to save on driving response time, an engineer had the bright idea of eliminating "neutral" in the gear system of his car. Needless to say, the car went from nowhere to nowhere very fast.

The Secret of the Butterfly

The butterfly changes not,
Of its own accord.

Deception

"Budo is cheating."

A playful mind and a playful heart are necessary attributes for surviving contradiction and paradox. We often spend our energies towards trying to solve a contradiction. It might be more useful however, to say that one needs to be happy in order to come to terms with what does not make sense. It's common for people to feel that contradiction and uncertainty are signs and proof that budo is not real. What is important to understand is that the tiny examples found in the dojo are nothing compared to the deception of the battlefield or of life itself.

To be geared towards only one avenue is to walk into a dead-end. Deception is the essence of all conflict, at least, for surviving it. Even a fair fight will be lost for the one that is eventually surprised. To be able to move from one extreme to another, without settling into either, is the heart of deceptive movement in budo. If one is able to change instantly as one should, then it is no stretch of the mind to understand how "what is" (a truth) can suddenly become "what is not" (a lie). This works both ways.

This interplay between truth and falsehood (kyojitsu) is the playground of the budoka. While the opponent is moving on one side of divide, the budoka straddles both.

> *"If the opponent can understand what it is you are doing, then it isn't budo."*

On a simple physical level, any opponent can punch, but if his fist contains a tiny blade, then his punch can suddenly become a cut. Moreover, he may not even hit you. He may just leave his hand out there in the air while you stare at it and kick you in the groin. The same is true for you. You may be in the midst of throwing somebody when suddenly you just stop and let them fall onto a curb. This is one way of denying the inevitable.

In one sense, the budoka is a cheat and a liar. Yet what battle was ever won with fair play? And when honor and morality do overcome the opponent, it is quite simply because the opponent was not prepared for it. Deception truly is at the heart of it all. Recognizing deception, the budoka allows it right of way. Some can only believe in lies. Some, only in truth. There are some, however, who can read between the lines and it is in between these lines that one finds real budo. If you can wait long enough for your opponent's truth to come true, then they will belatedly discover that they have deceived themselves.

> *"There is an interplay between reality and illusion, strong and weak, victory and defeat. It is here, between these things, where you are really strong."*

To delude oneself is the most common trick in budo. It is so easily done since the techniques for doing so are legion. To understand deception is to, basically, avoid deceiving yourself. Self-deception is probably the quickest killer on the battlefield. This works for you and against you. The interplay between reality and illusion requires a clear head, if not a clear spirit. Since budo is not about skill, strength or power, deception in budo is not a matter of you trying to outwit the opponent. Rather, deception in budo comes from the opponent. It is self-inflicting. The budoka does not need to engage in constant, intentional deception for the simple reason that the deception does not originate with him. What occurs to the opponent IS, quite literally, the opponent's fault.

> *"Unlike in sports, in budo you need to do foul after foul after foul. You need to be able to lie. This is kyojitsu. Budo is kyojitsu."*

One of the main differences between the sport martial arts and real budo is this: Rather than training to be powerful, the budoka trains to detect and avoid the power of others. The opponent's skill, strength and experience are forms of self-deception that work against him. As a budoka, your job, so to speak, is to avoid your own self-deception and to allow the opponent to destroy himself with his. If the budoka starts to believe in his or her own power, then their descent into self-deception has begun. The more you believe in what you think you know budo is, the more you will become trapped by that belief. Deception in budo works on a very personal level.

The interplay between illusion and reality is budo in motion. For those on the receiving end, deception is death. For the survivors, it is life.

"Beyond a doubt, truth bears the same relation to falsehood as light to darkness."—Leonardo DaVinci

Exchanges

I was the greatest exponent
Of truth until I learned
Falsehood.

I knew more than anyone
About reality until I discovered
Illusion.

And with everyone
Knowing more than me
I discovered the
Interplay.

Rocks sitting in gardens are exposed to all kinds of weather, from blistering summer heats to freezing winter colds. These garden rocks like to beleive that they are sensitive since they experience all of this weather but in reality, all they do is put up with it. Rocks don't experience anything.

Liar

Honesty cannot begin,
With self-deception.

Creations of Grandeur

A just spirit is the only thing
That will protect you,
From yourself.

The lights in the House of Darkness were on. A man with a flashlight walked in. He turned the flashlight on, switched off the house lights and then exclaimed, "I'm sure we'll find something now."

There was a man who once walked out of a second-hand clothing store wearing some new clothes he had bought. Walking with a swagger, he was overheard to say, "Wow, Emperor's Brand. How swish!"

Reality and Illusion

Living with either
Who of you will follow me,
Into the never land?

A man walked out of the shoe store wearing a pair of running shoes with spiked soles. With the spikes digging into the ground, each step was a labor as the man struggled to reach the front gate. Well before he had reached the gate, the man was overheard to exclaim, "With these shoes, I'll never slip!"

To Admit

Their illusion is truth
Their truth a dream
Their dreams the illusions,
Of children.

The Capacity

The fusion, bringing together
The expansion

What is next, was
And what was, gone

The interplay rolls on
Illusion, reality

And the dragon's breath
Breathing the coldest of fires

Warming those
Who warm themselves.

Whatever

Either or,
It makes no difference
To me.

"We all do 'do, re, mi' but you have to find the other notes
yourself."—Louis Armstrong.

Letting Go

"Letting go is the most important thing."

It is hard to accept that budo is something that we cannot possess. Though intimately part of the human experience, budo is in a very real way, not ours. You must accept that you cannot control it. You must accept that there is very little, in fact that you can control. You must accept that luck and chance rule. How strange it is that once you accept this, you will find your luck starting to improve. Luck is an integral part of budo. Its cultivation is one of budo's most unusual secrets. To train thinking that you will cover every possibility is to fly in the face of reality.

"You need to be good at finding lucky resolutions to each problem…the luckiest person will survive."

No matter what level of training you receive, no matter how advanced your weapons are, no matter how just your cause is, there is simply no guarantee you will survive.

If you can accept this terrible piece of bad news, then your chances of survival will drastically increase. Survival is the goal of budo, not winning and certainly not the glory of victory. Just survival…and that's all.

"Budo is for living, for surviving."

Being able to perform a technique in a fight means nothing. Being able to throw a shuriken in a fight means nothing. Fierce-looking fighting postures will not save you. Just because you started a technique does not mean that you need to finish it. You have to let go.

The need to hold onto something—forms, names, facts and figures, skills and experience—is very seductive. How many family names, how many civilizations, how many kings and emperors have fallen for the sake of "tradition?" Why were they never able to let go and simply survive? Survival is no small matter and if it ever seems like one, understand that things could change in the blink of an eye. Although many have, hopefully you will not be one of those who are willing to die to preserve their self-image.

It is terrifying, this thought of embracing uncertainty. But it must be done. We have to let go of our definitions, of our knowledge, of our contingency plans and tactical concepts. We have to let go of our skills and abilities. We have to let go of our rank and our power. Like a rocket streaking up into the night sky, we have to let go of what we do not need in order to keep on moving ever higher.

"Art is the elimination of the unnecessary."—Pablo Picasso

The path of the martial artist is often compared to the act of climbing a mountain. It is an apt metaphor. What they don't tell you, however, is that there is no "glorious view" from the top of the mountain. There is a gigantic, swirling darkness, a black hole, an absolute nothingness. The mountaintop is beautiful because it is alone, utterly.

What can you cling to in such a place?

"Some people never learn and they die.
Some are just unlucky and they die. There is
nothing you can do about it, but keep going."

1,000 miles

Know then,
That the dragon soars
Upon letting go.

Secret Places

There is a place where nothing can be found
Though everything exists.

The location of this place is secreted away
From where you cannot look.

And when you find this place
You will find nothing

That you didn't know before.

"Budo is not a technique, so a person watching
will not have any idea what is happening."

Surprises!

Walking on
I caught a glimpse of Eden.
I tell you
There was nothing there!

"Those of you who have been practicing basics for
20 years really should have let it all go by now.
You already know them."

"If you do not let go of thinking about forms, you will
not understand what I am showing."

A very strong martial artist boasted of his prowess at punching. He was famous for being able to punch flying birds. He was so successful at this that it wasn't long before the birds began avoiding him. He took it as a sign of success. Eventually, whenever he left the house, every living thing avoided him.

"It's important to let go and just let things happen."

It occurs to me that, since astronauts do most of their training underwater, that they ought to forget about space travel and just explore the oceans. There is nothing up there, anyway. Is there?

"It's important to find a 'lucky resolution' to these problems, to find that lucky movement."

There was a well known martial arts dojo downtown. The head instructor had been teaching for over 20 years. He had hundreds of students who came to his class each week and he was well known for teaching self-defense for men, women, and children. His most popular course was the Family Self-Defense Course.

"Anybody can be good at doing techniques; that's not really budo. In fact, it's irrelevant."

When you go fishing, you look for the best pools. When you bait your hook, you do your best. When you cast the line, you do your best. Once the hook hits the water, however, you have no control whatsoever over the situation. You must be patient and let both nature and providence take their courses. You can say that "you caught a fish," but really, the fish caught himself. He saw the bait, he opened his mouth and he took a bite. You had very little to do with it. The best fishermen understand this. The best fishermen don't even go fishing.

> *"Just let go. Let go of everything and*
> *watch what happens."*

In the jungle, only the monkeys admire the stars at night. Of the monkeys who admire the stars, only half understand that the stars are far away. Of that half, only half understand that they do not own the stars. Of that half, only half understand that the stars will endure long after their deaths. Of that half, only half understand that the stars do not care about the monkeys at all. Of that half, only half understand that the stars are terrible balls of destructive fire. Of that half, only half admire the stars at night.

> *"Don't go in with a plan. Let every*
> *attack be a surprise."*

How exasperated his critics must have been when, upon being told that a number of his works had been burnt out of misguided piety, the Australian artist Norman Lindsay replied, "Don't worry, I'll do more."

"What I'm doing has nothing to do with fighting."

A hunter walked into the jungle. He wore his talisman of protection, his best boots, carried two spears, a huge shikar knife and a big bore rifle. He dressed in green to match the bamboo thicket. He had stood over a fire to disguise his own scent with the smoke. He made no noises as he walked and he avoided traveling at the most dangerous time of day. His rifle was loaded and held at the ready. The tiger ate him.

*"You can't rely of the fact
that you're strong to
keep you from getting killed."*

Walk on fire, shatter glass, sleep on a bed of nails. I believe you have done all these things. I believe it took great skill and concentration. I would not do it, myself. I am too weak, too clumsy. I do have one question for you: That scar above your eyebrow, where did it come from?

Perched

Higher and higher I soared,
Intoxicatingly me!
Only to find that my feet,
Had never left the ground.

Santa Claus works very hard for 11 months a year, making perfect toys. Then, on the 12th month, he gives it all away and flies home with an empty sack, laughing and happy as he could be. How does he know all the children received a gift? Why is he not filled with fear, or apprehension?

One day, a young man decided to go to the dojo and learn how to defend himself. Using his credit card, he paid his tuition fees and bought a new training uniform. He was very excited about his decision to learn how to defend himself against any attacker.

The next day, an earthquake struck and destroyed the dojo.

Penance is the only way for a tiger to start anew.

"Don't be afraid to let go of the sword."

Pride

"I was trying to get bigger but
Takamatsu Sensei told me to be smaller."

The martial arts often attract proud, aggressive people with a need for authority and recognition. Budo requires a student to possess the opposite qualities.

Pride is a kind of disease. It must be cured before you can progress. A true master is not a doctor; he is a teacher of medicine. The student must listen to his teacher then diagnose and cure himself.

Success is dangerous in the martial arts. It gives rise to a belief in one's infallibility and a need to maintain that illusion. It also kills your budo, burying it where you think it stands. Pride among martial artists is like a broken neon light that stands out because it is dark. Knowledge, skill, strength, the many years of training— these are all kyusho (vulnerabilities) that breed the disease. Even if the martial artist has a reason to be proud, that pride works like a boa constrictor, choking the life out of its victim. How many martial artists recognize that they are their own victims?

*"Success is dangerous. One begins to copy oneself,
and to copy oneself is more dangerous than to copy others.
It leads to sterility."* —Pablo Picasso

Pride deafens, but the sound of budo is that of a whisper. Only the silent can hear it. This is no exaggeration. Look for the quiet ones. The loud too, often have something to teach but in the world of budo, it is the silent one to whom you need to pay attention. If you cannot silence yourself, then what will you hear other than your own shouting? The prouder the heart, the louder the heartbeat. How much can the ears of a proud heart hear? The only soldiers who believe in their absolute supremacy are suicide troops…

In this day and age it doesn't take much to be defeated. Guns and other such weapons have removed the handicap that the physically frail have often endured. Anyone can defeat you, even a child. (Perhaps even accidentally.) How many martial artists understand this? What does a black belt really mean to a man who knows his chances of surviving the drive home are only 50-50? You may be killed by a single microbe, a drunk driver, or an earthquake. What does it matter if it was an accident? A stray bullet will kill you just as dead as one that was aimed. How many martial artists understand this?

"Even a large man can trip on a small stone."

There is a concept in law called the "Eggshell Skull Rule." It says that if you injure someone, even if it was a gentle touch, and that person is unusually vulnerable (like an eggshell), you will be fully responsible for the consequences, regardless of your intentions.

We have to think of ourselves as eggs, vulnerable and weak.

Pride is one of the Seven Deadly Sins. For many, it is the most difficult sin to purge. Your belief in your own strength or skill will be your greatest weakness. Your knowledge of your own fragile vulnerability will become your greatest strength.

> *"A great man is always willing to be little."*
> —R.W. Emerson

The tiger is a beautiful animal. The pussycat is universally adored. Despite this, nobody hunts pussycats. It is the tiger, the beautifully terrible tiger that you will find in the hunter's sights. Do not make the mistake of thinking that budo is about becoming a tiger. If you see it as such, you will be hunted.

Budo is not yours—it is nothing to be proud of. Holding onto your pride, it will evade your grasp. Letting go of pride, budo will disappear. And when it does, it will speak to you. Budo speaks in a whisper; you have to be small enough to hear it. When you do, it will be the loudest whisper you ever heard.

*"Being strong in some way makes you weak
in every other way."*

Victory

*Watch them,
Seeking targets
So they can say,
They won.*

"It's difficult to become weak if you are strong."

Come ride the carousel, pick any wooden horse. They love the wind in their hair. The horses are frozen, painted and pretty. The move in a circle, they jump up and down, but they never get off, perfectly spinning along.

Once, there was a young man who had many friends. His friends used to love saying good things about him when he was with them but they also loved saying bad things about him when he wasn't. The man never found out if the bad things they said about him were true.

Sometimes, when you look around, you see people and you notice that they do not see you. They talk with you, they make jokes and laugh with you but they do not see you. Why don't they see you? How is it that you can see them?

Every day, a fine, strong donkey would walk past a huge, powerful river. He would stop and stare at his reflection in the water. It angered him that his reflection was unclear because the water moved so quickly, the ripples and waves moving and changing so often that he could not see himself clearly. "I will not drink this water," he said, "There is something wrong, something missing." He refused to drink and eventually, refused to even look at the river. He survived by drinking from a stagnant pool where the water never moved and his reflection was perfect and unchanging.

Animals are very clever. They may not have large brains like humans, but their senses are extremely acute and they are sensitive to every tiny sound and smell. Their instincts are finely honed from years of hard living. Put some peanut butter in a trap, however, and you'll catch one in a few hours. Traps don't exploit stupidity; they exploit desire.

"The strong tend to be straightforward and they are easily tricked."

There was a Cherokee boy named "Ten Horses" because he liked to scare the animals and make them stampede. He was proud of his name and often introduced himself to people who had known him since birth. His favorite thing to do was to stand upon a boulder and shout his name as riders on horseback dashed underneath him.

"I am Ten Horses! You have only one horse, but I have many!" He would walk home filled to the brim with satisfaction.

There was a small school for orphans and fools. The keeper was a kindly old lady. She showered her wards with praises and love, but a spanking was sometimes in order. When I went to the school (and this I don't understand) the proudest boys had red bottoms.

Glory Gone

The legions
Have thundered off,
Into oblivion.

*"Budo isn't a 'style.' Those teachers that put their own
ideas into it, they are just pieces of shit."*

There was a man who used to translate old European recipes into English so that people in America could experience some of their roots. He translated several whole books' worth of recipes. And yet, when he cooked for other people, it tasted terrible. People would ask the translator where he learned to cook. He claimed it was one of the old recipes he'd translated, but nobody could ever find it in his books.

Little children always show the truth, especially when they lie. How many chocolate-smeared lips have declared "I didn't eat it!?" How many parents could not see the chocolate?

Eight wooden Daruma bob their heads and bow. What big smiles they wear! What pride! What glory! The wood, the paint, they are all perfect! Come see them in ten years—they will look exactly the same.

**Gan Riki (Powerful Vision) by the grandmaster
—Masaaki Hatsumi**

Death

"If you are uncomfortable with death, don't come here."

Budo is killing. Make no mistake about this. Budo is not a self-improvement philosophy designed to make you a better person. It is not a social organization designed to help like-minded people connect with one another. It is not an athletic organization designed to improve the fitness of its members. All of that is fine and good and if that is all you can get out of it, then a wonderful thing has happened.

However, if you want to know the real budo, you cannot be exempted from the horror of what "living and dying by the sword" entails. You cannot understand budo if you restrict yourself to the same teachings that are given in children's classes. If you really want it, then you have to familiarize yourself with the human body and the exploitation of its fatal vulnerabilities.

You cannot shy away from thinking ruthless thoughts in the dojo. You have to practice every technique, every movement, with the idea that one of you is going to die. You need to be able to be the one who does the killing. If you are the one who dies, you need to really understand it. You won't get a second chance, you can't just go home and you certainly can't rely on the mercy of killers. You have to understand that you may not even see it or feel it. It might be a painless little flicker of a hidden razor across your neck.

"No matter how strong a person is humans still die."

One of the most difficult things to come to terms with is that budo comes from violence but budo itself is not violent. Another difficulty is the question of how you study something like budo during peacetime. This is an important question and its answer requires you to be receptive to someone who can share with you the feeling of the experience.

There are few who can pass on this feeling. When you do find someone who can, your acceptance of what they offer demands that you take full responsibility for your share of the blood and agony that you inflict. This is not a game. While budo itself is not violent, the results of it are and this creates a strain on the student that they must come to terms with. Understanding bloody knowledge requires you to take responsibility for the pain and death that generated that knowledge. This is the obligation we owe the dead.

The *densho* (scrolls) were written with their blood.

Violence is a horrible thing, ask any veteran. You must accept your portion of nightmares. There is a price to be paid for learning budo and the true martial artist will eventually come to realize this.

Musashi and other warriors wrote about the "resolute acceptance of death." He was not specific about whose death—maybe yours, maybe that of someone else.

"Budo was originally about taking heads. Later, people changed it into bowing and etiquette, but that's just a lie."

"Takamatsu Sensei taught me killing. He didn't teach me techniques."

One day, a mouse was being eaten alive by his friend, the cat. All the while, the mouse kept saying, "I'll have a talk with the cat. I'm sure we can work out our troubles when we have both calmed down." The cat thoroughly enjoyed his meal.

Heaven

I forced a glimpse
And saw the devil
Smiling back.

A certain group of doctors have been attending medical school continuously since 1980. When asked why they would stay in school so long, studying the same classes, over and over, it was discovered that these fifteen doctors had refused to take certain classes that "made them uncomfortable." The dean has made it clear that all students wishing to graduate must pass all of the assigned classes. The doctors insist, however, that they will eventually graduate if they just stay in school long enough.

Flame

In the world of demon truth
Liars burn under invisible flames,
The truth, protected,
By independence.

*"I'm not teaching you how to fight. I am teaching
you how to control evil. That's what
we are really doing here."*

A famous swordsmith was asked by a swordsman eager to learn the sword arts, to forge for him the perfect sword. The swordsmith agreed to the task and spent many nights laboring over it. Finally, after many sacrifices, the sword was finished and presented to its new owner who marveled at the calligraphy carved on one side of the blade. It read: "*With this blade, you will learn the ultimate secret of the sword…*" Thrilled with his new sword, the young swordsman spent years perfecting his sword skills. Much blood was shed in his quest for the secret of the sword until one day he noticed the calligraphy on the other side of the blade. It read: "*…when you sheath it and put it away.*" The swordsman went home and never drew his sword again.

Rifleman

*Wielding the new science
What fate will he not suffer?
His brothers, ages past,
Know all too well.*

*"Don't just stick him with it. Break the skin with
the sword tip, angle the blade and push it in.
We're not just killing frogs here."*

Proof

They hit upon it,
Every time they look over
Their shoulders.

"The lion is most handsome when looking for food."
—Jalal Rumi

I once had a friend who liked shooting, but she was very opposed to the idea of hunting, let alone shooting someone in self-defense. She would only shoot at the standard round targets.

"Shihan can mean 'great teacher' or it can mean 'the marks on a dead body.'"

Six Times

*I sat there, not knowing
But you were the Master.*

*Upon a summons, I rode the wave
And you caused mine.*

*Later, you would not let up
And I felt the fear of the edge.*

*The white light then stopped me,
And you asked me to follow.*

*I did, and when the time came,
The demon laughed, floating*

*Until now, the beginnings
And endings, of nothing.*

"Learning doesn't always feel good."

Living Between
the Lines

*"If it can be written down, then it's no good
in a fight. Real budo starts where words end."*

A budo master will teach what the scrolls do not reveal. How can he not? He IS the scroll. Words are just words. Real budo only exists in between the written forms, between that which is static. Budo is formlessness and constant change.

Do the scrolls contain all of the ancient secrets? Perhaps they do contain some hidden mystery, but if they do, then how they are read will depend upon the quality of the reader. Taking things at face value can be dangerous. If budo were the art of avoiding the dangerous, then accepting the scrolls as being the final, definitive truth would be suicide. You cannot learn budo by reading ancient scrolls! The scrolls are incomplete, vague and contain intentional mistakes. Imagine how far from the truth a translated version must be!

The scrolls—or anything written about budo—could be considered as a kind of screening mechanism. They separate the wheat from the chaff. Those that latch onto the meanings of the words become trapped. They can no longer move forward. Those who can step away from them continue on. With this in mind, budo words are like signposts; you don't get to your destination by staring at a sign, you have to keep moving.

"Don't be trapped by what you think you know about budo. The words in the scrolls are also traps."

It is natural to think that budo could be understood through the forms it takes. The written word is one such form. Physical performance is another. But budo is beyond the forms it takes. Budo is art and any art that is definable is dead. Art is life. It is an act of creation. Art is selfless and at the same time, infinitely personal. The supreme challenge in the art of budo is that you have to become a blank canvas and allow the opponent to paint a bloody self-portrait.

"People see a Picasso and they don't understand it, but they know instinctively that it is special. Real budo is like this."

To allow the opponent to be the brush with which you are painted; to allow yourself to be the clay that is molded by the opponent is a terribly difficult thing to accept.

"It is important to be able to see the abstract. You need to cultivate 'large eyes' for this. In time, you will learn to see what I see."

What good is a static form in a living world? You have to learn to live in between the dead forms. The waza (techniques) are like gravestones. You read them and learn from their mistakes, you don't use them to build a house.

When the grandmaster teaches, it is very rare that any of the recognizable techniques are seen. He is always moving in a way that cannot be understood. Some people on the outside perceive this as deception, but they deceive themselves! Others see what they imagine they ought to see. They create their own definitions of budo.

"You must be an artist to see these things."

Survival of the body—survival of the heart—requires us to avoid any rigid form and to deny inevitability. If you look for the grandmaster's forms, you will see nothing. If you look for his nothingness, you will see his form. This is art! Don't mistake these words for a riddle. This is literal truth.

"You will never become an artist if you are unable to see these things."

To live in an upright manner, to have a strong sense of morality and ethics, these are all wonderful things but the good do not always prosper and the bad often emerge victorious. It is important to understand the reality of lies and deceit. In a sense, budo is one kind of lie. And yet from this lie, beautiful truths are often born.

"You can't be fixated on any one thing.
In the Aesop fable of the ant and the grasshopper,
the grasshopper starves because he didn't work
like the ant. In reality, the ant could have
simply shared his food. There are no rules that
dictate what we can and cannot do.
This is how you negotiate infinity."

This Art

Where does it exist,
Except as a secret
In your heart?

Which part of the dough does the pizza man hold? Where is the handle? What is the diameter? How thick is the crust? It's not possible for me to make a pizza without this information.

"We must not think about what we will do,
only react properly to what happens."

Listening Fundamentals

What needs to be heard,
Is never spoken.

Apparently, two brilliant scientists have discovered what love is. They measured the biological responses of married people and discovered identical patterns in their biological responses. They also did a cost-benefit analysis of people who were in love and discovered an economic advantage over those who were not in love. Finally, the big question has been answered! We know everything about love now.

Mysteries

Gates closed,
In an open field.

"You must have the guts to throw away your techniques and move into the third dimension. I cannot teach you this; I only wish to share the feeling."

The only time art suffers is when you try to copy what you did before.

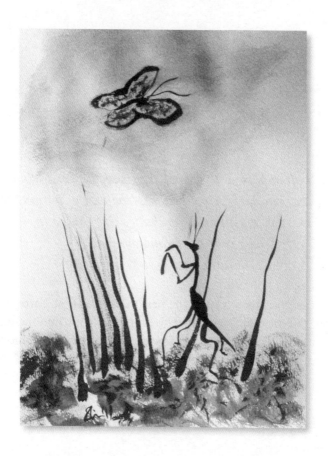

Earth has eight separate moons. It is a scientific fact. Today there is one moon and tomorrow there will be a different moon and so on, until the first moon reappears. Each one has a different shape and a different name. Every day, there is a new and totally different moon. You must learn them all or you will never know what day it is.

"Don't move like a martial artist."

Secret Message

Floating bottle,
You needn't arrive
At any shore.

"I often play with words, like Budo becomes Mudo
('the way of fighting' becomes 'the way of nothing').
You must be able to change like this with
your actual movement."

I can give you a map to the best fishing spot on Earth. I can show you the exact spot where to drop your hook into the water. I'll put it all down on paper. How can you possibly imagine that you might not catch a fish?

There were three ancient monks sitting outside an ancient temple, praying for enlightenment. They had been sitting there for many years, decades, in fact, of devotion. One day a young man approached the three ancient monks and asked them if they had yet received enlightenment. "No, it only happens in the brief moment before you die," said the oldest monk and the other two nodded in agreement. "Well, did you ever try going inside the temple?" the young man asked. "Oh, no, no," the oldest monk said, "no unenlightened person may enter."

Under the Blade

When nothing is left
Consider faith,
And the revelation.

"Budo can never be written down…Budo can never
be stolen…Budo can only be transmitted from teacher
to student, man to man."

Knowing how much training goes into a ballerina's skills, how every step must be perfect, how her arms and legs must move in the exact ways handed down through the generations, how even her fingertips must be under tight control, it seems amazing that they can walk through a parking lot and drive home.

Secret Knowledge

This is for you,
Magic is for the rest.

There is currently a trend towards 3D television technology. Many people are becoming excited by this new technology and the realism it promises. I wonder though, if any of these people notice the difference between what they see in the mirror every morning and what stands before it.

*"To read between the lines was easier than
to follow the text."*—Henry James

The Irony of Necessity

*Everything
Becomes nothing,
In time.*

*"No man is an expert because knowledge
is not static. The truth changes every day."*

There was an up-and-coming racecar driver who used to sit in wrecked vehicles at various parts of the racetrack for hours on end. He claimed that it was good preparation for a possible accident when racing. When asked "Do you think this will save you in an accident at 100 miles an hour?" he would frown and sit in the wrecked cars even longer.

*"Budo is feeling. If anybody says that the only way to
understand budo is by studying form, he is mistaken."*
*"The only difference between me and
a madman is that I am not mad."*—Salvador Dali

"You've become skillful.
You won't get better like that.
Try and have some fun."

Every year, the Tax Collector made his way unannounced to the King's Court in order to present the King and his Lords a summary of how much tax he had collected for the realm. And every year, during this presentation, the King and his Lords were absent while the Tax Collector pontificated on how much money he had collected. The Realm was very grateful for the Tax Collector's services—especially the Tax Collector.

"We must use the unknown spaces to survive.
In space, I move only myself and
in doing so, I move you."

Danger

"Even an insect can sense danger without seeing it."

Danger is a simple concept that anybody should recognize. In budo, you have to recognize it in the tiniest forms and you have to do so without relying on your eyes. It is common sense to see danger and avoid it. No animal survives for long without this ability. It may be, however, that we as humans have come to take it for granted that things are safe all the time.

They are not.

Since training is a relatively safe affair, we often tend to believe that we are not in any real, immediate danger. (This is the danger of confusing sport martial arts with budo.) The good student learns to recognize ANY POTENTIAL danger. Not many people seem to have this ability. Instead, many people require pain in order to recognize danger. That may be acceptable in the beginning, but the truth is, waiting for pain to indicate danger is a childish failure. The real thing requires sensitivity to what is coming, not what has already happened.

*"The scroll says to kick his knee,
but you could use a piece of pipe."*

When the teacher shows a technique with a punch, don't assume that his fist is only a fist. The worst-case scenario is not to be hit in the face. To be sensitive to danger is to recognize—and respond accordingly—that is the worst-case scenario. You have to assume that his fist contains a small razor blade. He may even have a small pistol in his hand, a tiny syringe, even thumbtacks. It's best to think of it like this: if he can touch you, he can kill you. The reverse is also true.

*"If you just choke him, then it's a sport,
like judo. We want to crush his throat or break his
neck and then choke him."*

Training in a slow manner seems counter-intuitive when talking about the violence of life and death struggles. But it is this kind of training that teaches you to be aware of the smallest dangers. How sensitive can you be to petite dangers when you are trying to kick and punch your way out of trouble at high-speed? If every kick and every punch you throw is being cut by an unseen weapon, you are only killing yourself. One should never let the study of techniques get in the way of recognizing danger to yourself or the opponent.

"It is no good if you cannot feel what is scary."

You can't wrestle your way out of a situation where the knife is already on your throat or the gun is in your face. You could try, (and you may even be successful.) but you must realize that you have already lost simply because you didn't recognize the danger in the first place. In a way, this ability IS budo; to sense danger before it can hurt you and to avoid it.

Recognize dangerous places, dangerous people, dangerous weather, and dangerous moods. You may not always have a choice, but awareness will mitigate the danger to you. In time, you may come to see that the difference between a knife and an icy road is only a matter of perception.

"When he attacks, grab a coffee cup and break it on the bridge of his nose, then grind his face into the broken pieces on the floor."

In learning to recognize what is dangerous to the body, one comes to also recognize what is dangerous to other areas of one's life. Budo is all encompassing. It touches upon all aspects of life. Danger doesn't only exist as a knife in the hand, an earthquake tremor or of a sense that the alleyway ahead is not the best place to go. There are more subtle dangers too, dangers that affect the spirit, the heart, and even the soul. To recognize how thoughts and ideas, theories and beliefs can negatively affect you is to enter into a new world. Ideas can be a form of poison. Belief too, so tightly held, can counter the grip and choke its believer. Not only can budo protect you on the outside, it can also protect you on the inside.

For sure, punching and kicking have their place but ultimately, the art of budo is to be open to what is damaging, on all levels, not only to yourself but to those around you, your family, your friends, and yes, even your enemies.

"You need some kind of danger
in order to develop."

Secret Lessons

By the looking glass
Looking to stay away,
From dangerous places.

There was an owl that used to fly in circles. Each night, he would leap from his perch and fly round and round and round. He knew all of the trees in his forest and was easily able to avoid them. Beyond his forest was a large land development project. Each month, the land developers would cut down the trees at the edge of the forest. Each night, the owl would fly in his circles, round and round and round until one day, there were no more trees left and the kids with slingshots who used to play in the parks of the newly developed housing estates took aim and shot the owl down for fun.

The lion is the king of the jungle. He has razor sharp claws, savagely long, saber-like teeth and an aggressive disposition towards any threat. He has no natural predators. And yet, pesticides are a common cause of lion fatalities.

A photo christened by the grandmaster as
Shinobi no Kabe—the secret wall.

*"It is more important to recognize what is
dangerous than to try and overcome it."*

There was a berserker who in his battle rage, would spin and spin and spin. With two battle swords in his hands, he became a deadly killing machine—nobody could stand in his way. He spun so much that he created a hole in the ground, slipped into it and never returned.

Remember how much of a shock it was to shake the hand of that crazy friend of yours who wore a hand buzzer? Yes, for just the briefest of moments, you got mad, didn't you?

Elephants have a mighty stomp—until they step into a hole.

Everyone has heard of the story of the scorpion wanting to cross a river on a frog's back. The frog was afraid of being stung during the trip, but the scorpion replied that if he stung the frog, the frog would sink and he would drown. When the scorpion did just that, he replied to the frog's shock that it was his nature to sting others. What the tellers of this story omit is that the scorpion's family had spent many a long hour trying to help the scorpion come to terms with his self-destructive behavior.

There was a punching expert who could smash his fist through many layers of wood. For years, he practiced his board breaking powers until his knuckles were so calloused that he could no longer grip his knife and fork and he starved from not being able to feed himself.

A Delightful Exchange

The words are mistakes that can get in the way of the magic.
"What words?"
The words people use when they don't understand.

"It's more important to not be there
when something bad happens."

The Empty Cup

"You have to careful. Often, what you see with your own logic is different from reality."

You must have a clear heart and a totally open mind to receive budo. Noble sounding words, indeed, but what does having an empty cup mean?

You have to be able to let go of everything you know about budo if you wish to learn from a budo master. These are words of great depth but what does "letting go of what you know" mean?

How can a student learn from a teacher when the student already believes he knows the lesson? In the beginning, it is normal to cling to "what you know," but budo is change. It moves. And what you thought it was one moment, transforms itself into something else the next. Rather than knowing what budo is, it is better to know what budo IS NOT.

It is hard to be totally open. To do so opens one up to the danger of believing in anybody. Naivety is a killer. Rather than an empty cup, perhaps we should strive to maintain a small hole at the base of our cup. Listen to everybody. Learn from everybody. But let what is an obstacle to what the master says and does drain out of that little hole.

It is better for the student to believe that what they know is wrong. In fact, in the world of budo, it is a certainty that what the student knows is wrong. It seems obvious, but for some reason, far too many people are unable to let the teacher teach. They keep their own ideas on a pedestal and no matter who the teacher is, his ideas often take second place. It is a ridiculous waste of time to only pretend to be a student. Consider the advice of a combat veteran with that of a recruit. In budo, the master is the boss. The question of being a student is also the question of WHOSE student you are.

Yes, it is true that the grandmaster once said we must "make budo our own." He did not say, however, that whatever we make up on our own is budo.

Imagine going to see the doctor, letting him examine you, paying him his fees and then ignoring his advice and discarding your prescription. Certainly there are differences between societies when it comes to questioning authority, but it doesn't take a genius to know when one needs to shut up and listen. People need to recognize when they are out of their depth. One doesn't rearrange the furniture when visiting someone else's house.

It is hard to let go of limits. What would opinions be without them! It is true that there are levels, both high and low. With time though, the distinction between these levels starts to disappear. What are we to make of those who cling to notions of high and low, advanced and beginner, good and bad? Beyond any limits, budo is a heart, a vessel that needs to be empty in order for the blood to flow. In budo, it is the heart that is important.

"Everything you have learned up
until now is nothing."

Some people look for inspiration from the master but it is hard to consider death and killing inspirational. Given that the grandmaster has always been very direct about what he is showing his students to do (and recover from), how someone would find this "inspirational" is somewhat of a mystery.

It is reasonable to believe that the grandmaster talks in riddles but by virtue of having gone through the fire, a budo master can only speak to you directly about what budo is. Understanding what budo is not is the student's responsibility.

If your cup is full, then hearing what budo is sounds a lot like what budo ought to be. For sure, we all bring our own ideas into the dojo but for the empty cup to appear, we have to let go, to let drain what we have brought with us. Remember, we go to the dojo to receive, not to give. This is *ukemi* (acceptance).

Lifeline

Healthy hearts
Pumping in,
And out.

There was an old man who fed hungry children all day. They would hold out their hands and beg. He would pull pieces of bread from an enormous bag and tell them to eat and be full. These children, being children, did not know they were starving; they thought they were just playing a game. They all had hopes of receiving a piece of chocolate. Every one of them, on the brink of starvation, would throw the unwanted bread on the ground and stomp it. "More bread please," they would say (because they knew if they asked for chocolate then the old man would give them bread out of spite.) But no matter how coy, they would always get bread and no matter how hungry they were, they would throw it on the ground. The old man kept feeding them anyway, his generosity and patience unmoved.

Dragon Wisdom

Beware the master liar
When you come before him
Seeking truths.

We all believe in something that is not. This is usually the province of childhood but fantasies often extend into adulthood. Is it right to say that the martial arts feed off this fantasy? That would depend on the student, of course, and the teacher. In the beginning, the world of budo is fantasy. In the beginning, that is all we have until one day, we encounter the truly mysterious. Being unable to penetrate into mystery, many of us persist with fantasy, defending it as the truth even unto God himself. Man creates fantasy, God creates mystery. Far too many teachers confuse one with the other.

Beginnings

There I was standing,
Waiting for heaven to open
But the only thing not closed
Was my mouth.

The rain falls every day somewhere on this planet. It covers the ground with the promise of life, but only if the deeply planted seed will drink. Only a good seed can drink the water and only a seed that has drunk will become a flower and rise above the dirt.

Muffled

The deaf ignore,
What they cannot
Hear.

"You must be able to hear and speak with your heart.
If you have some problem inside, then you will
not be able to receive budo."

"Sell your cleverness and buy bewilderment."
—Jalal Rumi

To Admit

Their illusion is truth
Their truth a dream
Their dreams the illusions,
Of children.

Remembering

I did not know what to do
Until I forgot to do
What I did.

Three pilgrims traveled to the Vatican. (To see the Pope, of course) They talked about themselves during their long journey. They brought pictures of themselves. They wrote stories about themselves. They were so happy the Pope got to see them!

There was a famous chef who had the most amazing talent. Every evening, a thousand guests would come over to eat at his banquet and every evening his wife would watch in amazement at so many guests satisfying themselves at her husband's table. After all the guests had left, she would ask her husband how so many people could leave so satisfied with his dinner. He replied, "Because I don't put anything on the table. That way, they can enjoy what they like."

A man with a full bladder hiked to a freshwater spring high in the mountains. He was too full to drink, but he had traveled too far to do nothing. So, he took lots of photos. When he was finished he went home, relieved himself of the water he took with him and shared his photos with his friends.

Phases

Speak, knowing the words
And then silence,
On understanding them

Sex and Feces

"Budo is comedy."

Budo is easily idealized. Some see it as a lifelong path of rigid self-discipline, one designed to forge the moral character of the practitioner. Others see budo as a kind of belief system, something akin to a religion, and confuse it with the moral strictures of such.

We are not priests.

Budo is many things to many people but most of all it is human. We miss something important when we divorce budo from stinking, hairy humanity and place it on a pedestal. Budo is blood and guts, semen and feces! The most natural way of dealing with such streng-verboten subjects (other than losing one's mind) is to laugh.

Some parts of budo cannot be understood without using the earthy metaphors and knowledge of sexuality, fecundity and the macabre. Humor is absolutely necessary! And, it has a deft touch (even when brazen). Humor scribbles its line between genius and insanity delicately and abruptly. Without its touch, we would all go mad.

Budo, as all art, is feeling. Feelings cannot be explained and descriptions can only ever be limited, but feelings can be shared. We all share human bodies and, therefore, similar lives. It serves no purpose to pretend that budo is separate from sex, food, fecundity, or any other aspect of human life. Whether you see it as being tragic or comical, more than one man has been assassinated on the toilet.

"Take his money after it's over. It's a donation."

Budo's dirty humor is one of its most common teaching tools. Of course, there is always a time and place outside of the dojo for crudeness, but inside the dojo, during training, there exists a state of liminality (an in-between condition wherein social rules are, for the most part, suspended). This is especially important for training properly.

In training, some people are afraid to touch certain parts of their opponents' bodies for fear of being inappropriate. Certainly, a sense of decorum and professionalism is necessary, but just because your opponent is a girl does not entitle her to train in the art of life-or-death combat without fear of having her breasts touched by a man. Your life is on the line! There is nothing out of bounds in the dojo. Never forget that budo is not a game and nobody is special.

"Squeeze him by the nuts.
If he squeals,
at least you know for certain it is a man."

We have to find a way to remove the embarrassing sentimentalities connected with such personal aspects of our lives in order to study and learn from them. Learn from your own weaknesses, habits, and pleasures. When you understand yourself, you understand the opponent. Think of yourself as an alien who studies human beings. Better still, think of yourself as a hunter. Hunters know when, where, and how animals sleep, eat, defecate, and breed and they exploit that knowledge efficiently.

Furthermore, budo requires a sense of play. "Demon Play" as the grandmaster calls it. You have to come to grips with your humanity and your mortality before you can play as he does. It's important not to be shocked by what one is capable of doing.

"Be a playful demon."

Last but not least, you have to grow up. If you can't handle the sight of an erect penis, a pile of manure, or blood and snot running out of a smashed nose, then you have no business learning how to kill.

Just as importantly, if not more so, is that fact that if you cannot find the humor in any of this, you will not be able to survive your own feelings when it's over.

*"If only one of us understands it will be enough.
It only takes one sperm to make a baby."*

In the hall of the king of the nine demons, there is a woman who has magical powers. No man can see her without feeling desire. The ripest, sweetest fruit is she. She will tie up your tongue and tie up your thoughts and tie up your hands with her eyes. Beware of this woman! She will tie up your soul and no girl will ever compare.

"Do it without grabbing, do it without touching....
Don't forget your evil laugh."
"You are all piles of shit, but through training,
a beautiful flower may grow."

A group of men were sitting around one day talking excitedly about their latest martial accomplishments.

"Did you see how many boards I punched through?"

"Wow, I never knew I could kick so fast!"

"I finished memorizing the defense forms!"

"That's great! I finished memorizing the attack forms."

"I'm sure my kicks are more powerful than yours."

"Maybe, but no doubt my punch is more penetrating than your kick!"

Throughout this exchange, one man, slightly older than the rest, remained silent. After a time, he got up to leave. When the younger men asked him where he was going, he replied, "Home, to make love to my wife."

"Women are very good at controlling men.
You're skilled indeed if you can control others
like a woman can."

Limits

As art, it is all useless
Without an artist.

"Go ahead and slap him.
Say, "You slut!" and slap him.
This is like a husband and wife fighting."

"First you get the feeling and then
everything else falls into place.
You have to watch every technique and
see the feeling behind it and the "killing way"
that could be added to it."

(the grandmaster had just demonstrated ripping his opponent's genitals off with a grappling hook. Everybody laughed but in reality, it would have been a horrific scene.)

The grandmaster once made a comment to some visiting journalists about the fact that there are transsexual people out there and you never know what sex they really are. The journalists laughed uncomfortably, not knowing why a martial arts grandmaster would discuss such an inappropriate subject in the middle of class. He then pretended to kick one of the students in the groin and said:

"If this person was really a woman,
my kick would have no effect.
If he looked like a woman,
I might not think to kick him in the groin."

"I'm going to my room to masturbate before
I have a light lunch, if you would like to come and
watch."—Salvador Dali

"You guys need to relax and lower your standards."

If you ever get chased by a big scary dog, don't hold back if it scares the shit out of you. The shit you leave behind may cause him to lose your scent in the trees. If you are being chased by a man, he may slip in the shit and hit his head on a rock.

"Ninjutsu means to persevere.
Sometimes that means persevering
with our own desires to do evil things."

There is a story about a leader who was photographed by spies having sex in a hotel room with several foreign prostitutes. When the spies presented him with the photographs and tried to coerce him, they were utterly defeated by his response. Instead of reacting with fear and embarrassment, the man swelled with pride and asked for larger copies of the photos so that he could share them with his friends back home.

"I don't hear any slapping,
so you need to do it harder.
That's right, slap the shit out of him."

How many "great warriors" throughout history have been brought down by a charming young woman? It happens every day.

Whoring

Dirty girl,
I forgot my soap.

"Wow! That's pretty good, isn't it?"

(the grandmaster was admiring a giant penis that he had painted for someone)

Secret Answers

Relish the confusion
Without hint of desire.
This is the answer,
To the question of sanity.

"This is like being a striptease dancer."

"Woman" by the grandmaster—Masaaki Hatsumi

Faith

*"Throw away your consciousness.
It is your consciousness that gets you into trouble."*

Belief is common. Faith, perhaps less so. Is it really enough to understand the teachings? Words are easily memorized and their utterance is easily confused for wisdom. If it is true that the highest levels of budo are available to any person, then it is also true that they won't be found in its rote learning. In other words, it is not enough to show up to a class and go through the motions by repeating words and movements. You must also believe in the reality of budo and commit yourself to it, irrespective of any doubts.

Of course, if you have any doubts—and any reasonable person may have doubts—then there is no shame in walking away from it all. The lessons of budo come from those who have given everything, usually unintentionally, to learn. However, if you do not believe in the reality of budo, then you will never progress beyond where you are comfortable.

For sure, there are degrees of understanding and acceptance in all areas of life and budo is no exception. It is one thing to believe in what you are doing. It is another thing altogether to believe that what you are doing is the totality. Budo requires a certain kind of commitment. To take a leap into the abyss is to leap into the totality. They call it a leap of faith for a very good reason; without faith, you cannot make it to the other side.

"There is something about budo that cannot be understood. It is transmitted and carried on. It comes from God and it is a light in the darkness."

Anybody can recite a prayer. Repeating the words of budo means nothing; the student must be able to move as his teacher moves and be judged so able not by himself or his peers, but by his teacher. This is where the silence of the master is at its loudest. When someone really understands, when somebody has faith, you will see it immediately in their movement. It will be like a flame that burns without revealing its source.

Of all the arts that people can study, there are none that require so much of a person as budo. If you are willing to sacrifice everything that you are in exchange for knowledge, and that is the cost, then it is reasonable to believe that what you are learning is legitimate. It is an interesting thing to see that many people who spend so much time and energy to learn budo have doubts about whether or not it is even real. Yet they keep training. They know, intuitively, that there is something here of great value. Without faith, however, they will never find it.

"You must have a sense for life and from this you are then able to put your trust, your faith, in your God and survive and live."

It would be a terrible frustration for us to look back on decades of training and to realize that we had missed out on the most important lesson because we didn't even believe it existed. Budo is right there! It can be glimpsed by anybody with the eyes to see. It can be accepted by anybody with the heart to do so. But you must be willing to do so. Your heart must be willing to accept what your mind may not. This is not easy and takes real commitment. Maneuvering your heart to match your thoughts is not the way to faith. You must do the opposite.

When the grandmaster moves, he does not move much. He does not need much.

Budo sustains him utterly.

Changed

**What have you done to me,
Demon Master?**

For some people, the budo-gi is a costume, for others it is a sign of respect, for a few others it is a sacred garment.

It was nearing midnight when a man entered the House of Darkness. The lights were on. Making his way over to a shelf filled with flashlights, he chose one, switched it on and exclaimed, "Now I'll be able to find my way around in here."

"Life is not a theory. Religion, philosophy, academia, all of this came afterwards."

"This is nature, natural justice. The flow of wisdom comes from God, through man, and into the world through our taijutsu."

Lambs

What did you sacrifice
In order to believe…
Faith?

"The chief enemy of creativity is 'good' sense."
—Pablo Picasso

Twisted by the Wind

Faith? No.
Just belief in more,
And more.

Three students sat next to each other on graduation day. They all had been hired by the same company for work after their graduation. Their teacher has asked them how they felt about starting work the next day:

Student #1: "I had a similar job before I started school. I'll just do things the same way I did before."

Student #2: "I am going to take night classes at another university to prepare myself for the job."

Student #3: "I am a little nervous, but I'll take it as it comes."

"Don't try and calculate what will happen next. Just go with it. These are things that are given to you by God."

Every year, hundreds of thousands of people flock to the Shrine of the Lady. Many of them make the last leg of the journey on their knees to show their thankfulness for the many blessings they have received. Some of them make the painful, expensive journey because the vendors near the shrine sell the best doughnuts in the world.

"Out beyond ideas of wrong doing and right doing, there is a field. I will meet you there."—Jalal Rumi

Faithful Heart

A reminder of,
Where strength lies.

A man, walking into his place of worship, was excited about the sermon he was about to hear. He had heard a lot about the holy man who was coming to speak and wondered what wisdom was in store for him and for the rest of the congregation. Arriving, the man stepped inside and found the hall empty.

"Don't play what is there, play what is not there."
—Miles Davis

Joy

"Develop your natural instinct."

Despite all of the fear, loathing, horror, and disappointment that budo can cause it is also a source of joy and fulfillment. It would be a mistake to assume that "joy and fulfillment" means only "happiness," although that is certainly a part of it. There are many kinds of joy in budo. They won't come quickly or cheaply. Budo starts out fun, then it becomes confusing, then horrifying and finally, all three at the same time. All three contain joy. In the end, you won't feel anything about it at all except joy. It will just exist and you will understand that existence without needing to judge it.

There is an unspoken source of joy in budo. It is something that very few people can admit to themselves, let alone admit to others and only rarely is it discussed. If you are human, then in some dark corner of your soul, you have a love of killing. There is no word to describe this exact passion; most of the words that come close imply a mental illness in a person; Sadism, schaden-freude, epicaricacy, etc… Many words are used to describe this character "flaw," but it is a well-established fact in psychological literature that the vast majority of soldiers experience a profound pleasure in killing; a pleasure on the magnitude of sexual release or the consumption of narcotics. In fact, studies suggest that cases of Post-Traumatic Stress Disorder occur more often in soldiers who were in battle but never got the chance to actually kill. They also suggest that it is the struggle to overcome inhibitions against such behavior that induces illness. Face it, accept it without judgment and let it become a strength or it may eat you alive one day.

"If you cannot let go of the killing act, of causing damage, then you will develop problems later on."

Accepting the fact that some have already died and that we too will die is another duty of the martial artist. It is truly a paradox that one can find joy amongst graves. It takes a very mature person to do this. No one can explain how it comes about; it is unique to every person, every heart. True joy can only come from an unclouded view of the world. You see the good and the bad and everything else. Some people are blessed with such powerful vision at birth. Most of us have to suffer the slings and arrows of long life and reach this stage only in our golden years. If you go to war and survive, you may come to see it while you are still young.

Like a full-body tattoo, it seems like there will be no end to your self-inflicted suffering. It takes time and a willingness to throw away cherished but unnecessary parts of yourself, but eventually it will come, and fear will leave you like a fever after a prolonged illness. Once you catch the Feeling of budo, training will no longer feel like combat, but more like a happy, impromptu dance. The Feeling of budo is unmitigated joy; a "dance of unexpectedness."

"This year's theme is to find your place, your nature, and to learn to smile and forget about budo."

There will come a time when the only thought in your heart is gratitude. It is an intensely humbling feeling. It comes from having passed through the suffering that created budo. You will be able to differentiate between this *majime* (sincere) gratitude and the more common one by virtue of the fact that the question of "Why me?" becomes "Thank you for letting it be me!" The fortune of life becomes clear. In budo, one lives by surviving and by surviving, one lives. This is a deep secret and its source is persistence. One maintains courage in the face of change. This courage, after a time, becomes change itself.

Some people never see anything but morals and virtue in the martial arts, but rest assured, they are like stones skipping across the surface of a very old and deep river. The stone that sinks to the bottom will drown in the darkness. It seems impossible to imagine that a person could find joy in that terrible place, but budo is the art of self-resurrection.

You will die and be born again and you will float out of the river and into the clouds.

Payment

Oh God,
The cost!

How to catch a monkey: Put something the monkey wants inside a jar or a gourd. The monkey will reach inside and take the bait in his fist. The monkey, unable (or unwilling) to let go of what he has grabbed, will be trapped and very unhappy.

Asunder

Divide yourself,
And become one.

"You don't want to be always killing. This is a kind of illness. Budo training is a way of curing this illness."

One day a lizard was found rolling in the dirt, clutching his belly, laughing uncontrollably. When his wife asked him what was so funny, he said "look at my ass!" His wife did so, only to find that his tail was missing. "A crow tried to eat me today," he continued, "but all he got was something I don't need and I am still alive!"

An orgasm is a buildup of desire. If your desire builds up for too long, you will feel pain but once you let it all out, nothing. Sweet nothing.

Original Man

You have reason to fear,
He who would witness
His own resurrection.

"You don't need to be a genius or a master for this."

Movement

Virgin jungle
And hidden cries,
For life.

"Life goes on even if you don't understand."

"Become aware of your own existence."

Did you hear about the story of the soldier who returned home from the battlefield? He promptly forgot about everything, got married, raised a few children and lived a wonderful life with his family. You won't find his story in the history books though.

Ninja Weapons

"Weapons are expensive. A modern fighter jet is very, very expensive."

One of the most interesting parts of budo, the study of weapons, is also a study in desire, inhibition and spontaneous creativity. Weapons usually suggest to a person how they should be used. You see the sword; you recognize that it has a handle and a cutting edge. You pick it up by the handle and you desire to cut with the edge. Reasonably too, one sees that A leads to B leads to C…

Ninja weapons defy this conventionality. Choke with the sword, cut his throat with a teacup, break bones with the rope, grab with the knife, paralyze with a ball point pen. Conventionality is not an aspect of the weapons themselves; it is an aspect of the user. Some weapons, like the *shikomi* (sword cane), do help us see how things are not always what they appear to be. You have go way beyond that understanding. You have to ignore all the conventional assumptions and embrace a totally unlimited, unconventional way of thinking. If you can do that, then any object becomes a "ninja weapon." This is an example of the *kihon happo*, the "infinite paths" of budo.

"It doesn't look like much, but that is why it is dangerous."

There is something more. Like a particle of antimatter, ninja weapons only "exist" for a few moments and then they disappear. They do not exist until you enter Kimon, the Demon's Gate. Kimon is the place where the enemy is vulnerable and you are safe. When you leave Kimon, the weapon ceases to exist. You cannot enter Kimon by using a technique. It just happens. This is why what we call ninja weapons are not "used" per se. They simply enhance the possibilities of that terrible moment. The tiniest things become terrifying and devastating because they are not openly, intentionally or purposefully directed towards the enemy. They only pop into existence during that moment when the enemy is ultimately vulnerable to something tiny.

One might say that real budo is the art of witnessing an accident.

It is important to understand that what is considered a ninja weapon was not limited to the ninja. Anyone, from any country, culture or period in history who has survived, even by accident, has made use of ninja weapons. Survival knows no barriers. Consider that ninja weapons represent a state of mind. It may even be better to forget about the word "ninja" even. Just stay alive.

Once the fight is over, you have to let go of fighting. To keep your sanity after a conflict, it is easier to lay down your weapons as if you were never holding any. We still have to live once we survive.

"I can change because I am not holding on to anything."

Dragon Stepping

Move with ignorance,
Total knowledge.

A man walked into a train station with a briefcase in one hand and a pencil in the other. The train would not arrive for quite some time and the man was feeling drowsy. So, he bought a cup of coffee and took a seat. He laid his briefcase across his lap and placed his coffee cup upon it. He used his pencil to stir the coffee. When he was done, he threw the coffee cup away and went to work.

When they cut Jonah from the belly's whale, they found in his tightly closed fist a few ounces of uneaten fish food.

"The ninja was the strongest because he wasn't limited
by conventional ways of using weapons. He didn't just
cut and slash in stylized patterns. He'd throw his sword,
even if it was a long sword. He'd flip it into the opponent,
whatever. You must keep this in mind. You never know
what will happen."

There was a Russian fighter pilot in WW2 who survived a dogfight by out-flying the German plane on his tail. He flew his fighter so fast and close to the ground that the German pilot clipped a tree and crashed in a ball of flame. When he was asked why he didn't just try to shoot down the German, he replied, "I forgot I had guns."

Hazy Shade of Wisdom

Confusion sets in
When the tiger roars,
In silence.

"You never know how bad things might get, so don't start shooting your gun until you have to. Use it in other ways as much as you can and save your bullets for emergencies."

"If you try to use a weapon, you will be no good."

Hans Brinker was a little Dutch schoolboy. He did not carry tools for plugging dikes, he did not know when a leak would occur and he did not walk in a special way, anticipating a leak. He certainly did not condition his fingers in anticipation of disaster. He was simply taking cakes to a blind man. But at the precise moment of necessity, an eight-year old held back the enormous power of the ocean itself with a single finger and saved his country from devastation.

"Put your thumb inside the teacup when you smash it on his face so that you can keep one of the pieces. Then you can use it as a shuriken."

A drunk, staggering through the street, trips over himself and he stumbles onto a mugging. As he falls, the wristband of his watch snaps, the watch flies off into the air and strikes the mugger in the eyes and temporarily blinds him. The mugger's would-be victim falls over and his shoes slip off, which hit the mugger under the chin. As the mugger falls back, the drunk collapses on top of him, knocks the air out of his lungs and falls asleep on the now unconscious mugger. People pass by and throw coins at the display. One of the onlookers comments, "Now that is what I call busking!"

"Art is a lie that makes us realize the truth."
—Pablo Picasso

Creation

What is this thing
That has nothing to do
With you?

"There is life in the weapon. Through that, you can live."

Hell

Before Heaven,
Swords rise and fall,
At will.

Buyu and the Dojo

"Budo has nothing to do with making friends. Budo is a solitary thing. People confuse friendship for budo."

I was sitting in the dojo one day, watching a demonstration. Suddenly, I became curious about what the grandmaster was doing. I turned around only to see him grinning and holding a sword inches from my head. His laughter, for a time, distracted me from the fact that I was dead. In hindsight, I shouldn't have been surprised. This is budo.

"A dojo is a place for confession."

The dojo can be many things to many people. For some, it is a social club. For others, it is an arena for competition. In some arts, the dojo is even seen as a place for business networking.

Be that as it may, the grandmaster has said that above all, the dojo is a place for confession.

"A real dojo is wherever you are."

Budo is a solitary pursuit. Though you may find yourself in the midst of seemingly likeminded people, their presence does not constitute a dojo. You must always remind yourself of what it is you are doing in front of your teacher. In a very real sense, the dojo is just you and him.

The deeper significance behind the term "dojo" is often lost. The word is generally translated to mean "training hall." However, the kanji characters that make up the word dojo literally read, "path-place." Perhaps we are better off understanding the characters as "A place on a path." If the dojo is with us at all times, ought we not to consider then that perhaps we are the dojo?

If you look at budo as a means for coming to terms with your own innate brutality, then the dojo IS a place of healing. The grandmaster's admonishment to treat the dojo as a confessional is perfectly valid and appropriate. Budo (and budo is human) is made up of some nasty things and it is necessary to heal oneself of that nastiness. That means it is your responsibility to seek out the place of healing and it is your responsibility to do as the doctor instructs, not only in the hospital, but everyday, everywhere.

Buyu, our budo brothers and sisters, are people you train with. They are also our teachers. It is not uncommon for us to become very close and to develop strong bonds of trust. It is a wonderful thing. That does not mean that you won't have to kill them one day.

"The dojo is like a hospital. You're here to be fixed."

This is a necessary concept: When you train, it is kill or be killed.

You may be among friends, but not really. You have to think of your training partners and your teachers as killers. If you are enjoying class because you are spending time with friends, then you are missing something. Your training partner is trying to kill you. Your teacher is trying to kill you. It may be training, but if your mind isn't in the right place, then what are you learning? You have to believe that he is trying to kill you. (And if someone has accidentally left a real sword in the rack, he MAY kill you.) This is one of the "weird" parts of budo: we kill the ones we love (not physically, of course).

When class is over, you can be friends again, but it's never really over. There is something else you need to consider: Every person's understanding of budo is his or hers alone. Even if you have trained together every step of the way, every budoka trains alone.

Your understanding of budo, as it comes to you from the Grandmaster, takes precedence over the opinions of friends.

"You have to be able to see things for yourself. Not just believe what someone else has told you."

Budo is an independent study. You will go through a stage where you may appear aloof and distant, with everyone around you being "wrong." It takes time to work through this phase. It also takes courage to be able to stand alone. To walk into the dojo supported by the opinions of your peers is one thing, but to walk into the dojo supported only by the lessons of your teacher is another. If you can do so, consider it a sign that you have been promoted.

> *"Painting is a faith, and it imposes the duty to disregard public opinion."*—Vincent Van Gogh

It is hard to separate friendship from budo and many people become trapped in confusing the two. Those that can make the distinction are blessed in finding true friendship, but make no mistake: Budo is a very lonely road. You must persevere and continue on. Understanding budo is a terrifying thing, but it may eventually lead you to joy.

> *"You are alone in the dojo."*

Once, a young man invited a friend of his to help prepare for some demonstrations that were to be held at an upcoming festival. Making their way to a local field they began practicing. Hour upon hour the young man was helped by his friend in perfecting his part of the performance. Finally, satisfied with his work, the young man decided to go home. On the way home, he turned to his friend and said, "Oh, we forgot to practice your demonstration." His friend turned to him and said, "Yes, I know."

*"You want to get together with good people and train.
This is important."*

Speed Bumps

*They, whom they look up to,
Are standing in their way.*

His chest sticking out, the young man walked up to the old man, and with a smirk greeted him, "Hello, long time no see. How have you been?" Before the old man could answer, the young man continued, "You don't have to answer. I'm younger than you." The old man looked at him for a moment, then looked away. The young man stepped in front of him and asked, "How are things with you?" And as before, the young man continued, "You don't have to answer. I'm younger than you." The old man turned away and then disappeared. Still smirking, the young man mumbled, "It doesn't matter, I'm younger than him." As he walked off, he never noticed the old man resting on his shoulder.

*"Be able to put your humanity aside and
become a monster if you need to."*

Two prisoners spent 10 years in the same cell. They became very close friends, sharing every thought. Eventually, one of the prisoners was informed that he was being released. His cell-mate screamed, "You can't go! I have 5 years left on my sentence!" His cellmate walked out the door.

"When it comes to art, more than having a teacher, you must be able to learn by yourself. In budo though, you need someone who has the experience of the feeling of killing. This is the difference between budo and other arts."

"Sometimes you may have to sacrifice your partner to win…Remember the Alamo."

Shared Experiences

Private, solitary,
Unknowable.
This is the nature,
Of this art.

"Think of him not as your opponent, not male,
not female, not even as an enemy. Don't have any
personal relationship with the opponent at all.
Just play with 'it' until the end."

Mushin, Zanshin, and Kyusho

"Many people are fans of budo, but are not budoka."

The martial arts are very interesting. Through it, you can find a love for exotic weapons, techniques, history and spirituality. Even words are not exempt. It is always an odd experience to hear, for example, an English speaker use non-English words to describe the most simple of things. Instead of using the words "hand guard" or "scabbard," one often hears the words *tsuba* or *saya* in their stead. This desire for things exotic can be a kind of blinker for some people.

Mushin

Mushin is probably the single most well-known and yet totally misunderstood concept in the martial arts. It is not, however, a state of non-conciousness, but the total opposite. It is a state of actively denying the self and refusing to make any plans in any immediate moment for the future.

That might sound hard to understand, but if you have plans like kata in your mind, how on Earth can you respond to the unknowable future? You have to remain undecided even after the fight is over. At first it may seem like a day dream, but once you get your desires and ego under control, you may shake with effort, during training, because your own desire to perform pre-ordained movements will be so strong. Forget Kata! Just Be There and move like a puff of smoke in the wind of your opponent's intentions. The attack will tell you were to go (which is *kimon*, the demon gate) See how it all fits together?

> "Mushin *is often translated as 'no mind.'*
> *However, it can also mean natural or unplanned.*"

Zanshin

Zanshin is much easier than the rest. It simply means that victory will be your most vulnerable moment and you can't let your awareness of danger leave you even if you do survive. A simple way of looking at zanshin is to have any random person attack you from behind while you are training with someone else, preferably at the exact moment when you think you have won.

"Zanshin can exist after war and it is not always a pleasant thing. Imagine seeing a mushroom cloud."

Kyusho

Kyusho (well-known vulnerable points on the body) have long held captive the imaginations of martial artists and fans of kung-fu movies. If you have been reading closely thus far, then you may guess what is coming next. (Constant change and the spontaneous winking-in and out of existence) In the true budo traditions, Kyusho are not necessarily stationary points on the body, to be searched for and exploited like cities on a map.

Like ninja weapons, they can be spontaneously created by circumstances. For example, a very strong part of the body, if twisted or stretched, may become very weak and vulnerable. These things will happen if you are patient (as in "perseverance" you know, the 'nin' in ninjutsu? blossoming like a beautiful red lily just for you.)

"This is not something created by humans. It has to do with the spirit. Remove yourself and be courageous in your consistency in the spaces between."

"The kyusho flow, they are not set."

In WW2, more pilots were shot down when they are on the tail of an enemy plane than at any other time. Winning itself is not a defense to another attack.

There are always at least two players in a game of roulette: The gambler and the ball. Everybody knows how the game is played. They know the numbers and the wheel, the colors and the rules. Despite all of this, nobody knows what the winning number will be.

And yet, the ball always lands on the winning number. How does it do that?

Zero Point

*Consider the absurdity
Of nothing and the obvious.*

A mama bird was busy feeding her hungry chicks. Each chick would open its mouth at random intervals to take another bite. She did not know which beak would open next, so she just kept her beak somewhere in the middle of the nest. The mama bird was very busy, cutting up pieces of the worm and placing a piece in each little beak as it opened. She didn't try to force open any closed beaks, she merely waited for a beak to open, over and over again.

"I'll play it first and tell you what it is later." —Miles Davis

The difference between budo with *mushin* and budo without *mushin* is the difference between Picasso and "paint-by-numbers."

99.9999999999999% of an atom is empty space. The only reason it seems solid is because of its connection to other atoms. The atom spins and vibrates at incredible speeds without ever going anywhere.

If you have your antenna tuned in correctly, you can pick up the faintest signals from space. But if your tuning is off by just a fraction, all you get is white noise.

A man walked into the House of Darkness to purchase a flashlight. Turning the flashlight on, he walked out of the darkness staring at its light while all the while mumbling to himself: "The light is so bright, I can't see anything."

Soap bubbles are so much fun! They float around, forever eluding our grasps. When you think you've got hold of one, it disappears only to be replaced by another, and another. They are everywhere!

Wounds

Foolish man,
Swords cut, even if
You do survive.

Selfish-Awareness

You never counted
On your own reckoning,
Did you?

These Words

These are the words
A revelation, revealing.
Would they be read
With one part of six
Or with the whole
That sustains?

These are the words
An awareness, aware.
Would they be known
Without your knowing
Or with the knowledge
That weighs?"

These are the words
A silence, silent.
And they will be heard
Not as clamor and braying,
But with the stillness
That moves.

"There may always be somebody else.
It's never really finished."

Perfection

"Perfecting the forms is for beginners."

Long accepted as being the goal of martial arts study, many martial artists persevere for years to perfect techniques, skills, and weapons. A further struggle is the perfection of the self. Manners etiquette, philosophy—a great deal of effort is spent on becoming perfect, even if only in some small way.

Perfection has a ring of nobility to it. "Mastery," "perfection," "flawlessness" are all commonly stated values in the martial arts. Its attainment is an admirable goal, to be sure, but one must never lose sight of the fact that budo is formlessness. Once you make it—or force it—to exist, it disappears. Is it wrong to say that chasing after an impossibility is the same as chasing after a fantasy? How elusive perfection is! And little wonder. It doesn't exist. At least in budo. The more you chase after it, the more it stays away from you.

"Have no fear of perfection—you'll never reach it."
—Salvador Dali

The seeking of perfect form is not budo. A perfect looking form may look good and be personally satisfying, but this has more to do with the desires of the practitioner than with budo. Not only that, it will never happen. A person could easily spend their whole life (and many have) trying to achieve this perfection. And if you ever should achieve it, which would indeed be a fantastic feat, it would still not be budo.

"Do not try and think of working for perfection.
If you try and work on this, you will never improve."

Budo is not much more than a series of mistakes and the budoka changes with each of these so-called mistakes, moving into a free flowing world where the artist finds his space. These mistakes rarely appear as things of beauty; budo often looks ugly and gritty. It is hard to equate beauty with ugliness but that is one of the talents of the budoka, to be able to recognize this beauty when human constructs fail.

"Don't think about perfecting your punches and such.
Study how mistakes are a normal thing and to
not be flustered by them."

For the athletically or spiritually minded, doing budo correctly often results in a positive feeling when finished. The athlete's satisfaction after a hard training session or the intellectually stimulating discovery of more principles is a common one. But budo is not a sport nor is it a theory or philosophy. In the beginning, doing budo correctly will not make you feel good when it is over. There is no rush at the end. If it's for real, your first feeling may be guilt, even if it was necessary to save a life. Nobody will be complimenting you on your form. More likely, they will be putting you in handcuffs until things get sorted out.

"Ninshiki wo shinobu"
(Endure the realization [that we are killers].)

The seeking of correct, perfect form can be an obsession with many martial artists. Indeed, many martial arts are concerned only with it. Perhaps the seeking of forms has its purpose. After all, the ability to narrow your focus onto performing a strict set of forms can be an effective way to manage stress. But is that budo? For those who have been in the military the question needs to be asked: What part of basic training did you find to be effective at relieving stress?

Perhaps the most common rationale for perfecting martial arts forms is that once they are perfected, they can then be let go of, thrown away, as the saying goes. This seems reasonable but after ten, twenty, or even thirty years of training in these forms, one has to wonder: how long does it take to be able to let go?

Techniques certainly have their place in budo. But keep in mind the old saying: "Never take a knife to a gun fight." Someone will always have a gun, no matter how sharp your knife. So why then are there even techniques in the martial arts? Consider the answer to that question like this: Techniques are studied in order to learn budo. One does not study budo in order to learn techniques. And what does this study entail? Learning to let go of the need to study techniques...

It sounds almost ridiculous to say that one studies something in order to realize it is not necessary but that is the way things go. We often spend our formative years learning the difference between black and white, only to discover that in the real world, there happens to be a lot of gray. Budo and the desire for perfection can be seen in the same light.

Perfection is a beautiful concept. It has inspired many to perform fantastic feats of elegance, grace, and beauty. But budo is life, complete with all of its gritty little mistakes, miscalculations, and frustrations. To go beyond the idea of what we deem is beautiful and to enter instead, the world of what is there, is to leave the crutch of perfection behind and to embrace life.

"Budo is a living thing, always changing.
People who don't understand this are just "technique
collectors." That is not budo. A great pot-maker
would give his pieces away or throw them into
the sea when they were finished. They were no longer
precious to him. That is the feeling of true budo."

Icemen

Some solidify liquids,
Thinking themselves
Masters of the flow.

When children play, there is mud and dirt, laughing and crying; the building blocks collapse, the crayon colors never stay inside the lines... what part of a child's play is perfect?

*"I am teaching you how to play...
to play as demons play."*

"Kanpeki de ha nai, dakara, kanpeki"

(It's not perfect, therefore it's perfect.)

Two lost, hungry boys found an entire box of cookies by the side of the road. All but one of the cookies were broken into pieces. They spent all day arguing and fighting over the perfect cookie. The next day, one of the boys made it home.

*"I want you all to capture the feeling of play
in your budo."*

The shark is one of nature's most perfectly formed creatures. Its body design allows it to almost effortlessly roam the oceans in search of prey. Sleek, silent and savage, the shark is absolutely hopeless out of water.

"Basics are said to be important, but they are not actually used in a real fight. Real fighting is always a case by case situation."

Racer

Breakneck nothing,
All the way to
Nowhere.

*"Don't give your opponent anything.
Control him with nothingness."*

How frustrating it is for adults when they cannot catch hold of a floating balloon, while for children, it's all part of the fun!

"My life has been nothing but a failure."
—Claude Monet

The purpose of camouflage is not to look like a soldier: it is to NOT look like a soldier; to look like sand or leaves and dirt, formless, shapeless, nothing.

*"There are various kinds of arts. The judge of most of
them is often the public. With budo however, good
budo has nothing to do with the average person.
This is a difference between budo and the other arts.
The person watching cannot see."*

Three men are sitting around a table. There is a glass of water.
One man says, "The glass is half empty!" The second man says,
"The glass is half full!" The third man reaches over, drinks the
glass and then gets up and leaves.

The Nature of the Vessel

*I would like to write the most beautiful of prose
There would be no letters in this prose
No words or sentences.*

*I would like to paint the most beautiful of paintings
There would be no brushstrokes in this painting
No shapes or colors.*

*I would like to recite the elegant of poems
There would be no words in this poem
No sounds or emotion.*

*I think only then
With nothing else but me
Could I call myself and artist.*

"You are not able to do this because you're trying too hard to do each little part perfectly."

A man complained angrily at the pet store one day. He kept saying that all the fish tanks were empty. "They're not empty," said the manager, "we just took down the labels for cleaning."

Still very angry, the man replied, "How can I see any fish if I don't know what to look for?"

"Do not fear mistakes. There are none."
—Miles Davis

Teaching

*"Don't worry about teaching;
you don't need to be teachers."*

It has long been assumed by many that becoming a teacher of the martial arts is an inevitable phase in a budo "career." Some people think that because a person achieves a certain rank, they must begin instructing others. Others feel that teaching budo is the only way to understand it.

*"I can't teach you this.
You have to do it on your own."*

Teaching requires a syllabus of sorts, even if only an unconscious one. And many teachers, working from such a syllabus, have a need to believe in its authority and through this, their own authority. It is a very easy matter for a student to also believe in that authority. This is a dangerous thing. Budo is a kind of "nonknowledge." The less you know of it, the more likely you will understand it and you will come to realize the impossibility of teaching something that can only be learnt.

Budo is change. It is replete with contradictions and paradox. Its blueprint is life and death but those martial artists who fall into the trap of developing the authority and prestige of being a teacher are failing to follow one of the natural rules of budo that is to not show what you know. Blueprints, curriculums, syllabi; these all work to eliminate change, to solve contradiction and to remove chance from the picture. But this is impossible. A martial artist who "teaches" has already stopped learning, no matter how skilled, talented, or charismatic.

"Never be a teacher. When you are a teacher, your budo dies. Always be a student and never think you are good."

Anyone can teach you how to replicate a physical form. Punching, kicking, rolling—these are all simple enough acts that anyone can teach and anyone can learn, and there is nothing wrong with that. However, budo is infinitely larger than this. If you can only teach what is visible, then you are only teaching a tiny, tiny portion of budo.

If you can only teach a tiny portion of budo, you may be tempted to believe that what you are teaching is the totality.

You might also be tempted to believe that the part of budo you can't teach is only achievable by "mastering" the parts of budo that you can teach.

This is not meant as a criticism of all teachers of the martial arts. but it is important to encourage a different understanding of what being a martial artist can mean.

It is very difficult for people to relinquish positions and feelings of authority. Stating humbly that one does not understand is not the same as actually believing it. It is in this way that teaching can be a very dangerous trap.

"I am not teaching you so that you can teach."

Budo is a solitary pursuit. It is a man-to-man training. There could be a thousand people in the training hall but if you are truly listening to the master, you are his only student—even if the other 999 people in that training hall are truly listening. Real budo training only needs one student. With that in mind, the idea of teaching in budo clearly becomes anathema to real learning.

A person training may influence others and may even attract others towards him. At this stage, a real teacher would simply continue on, irrespective of who passes through his orbit. Many gravitate towards the limelight and, in doing so, suffocate the life of their learning. A real teacher must let go of being a teacher. To the casual observer, there is little indication of who is who. Above all, a teacher needs to be able to hide.

How many pupils did Michelangelo have? What about Monet or Van Gogh? It is clear then that art cannot be taught. For sure, there may be some rudimentary physical actions involved but the spirit of art cannot be taught. It can only be nurtured by not interfering with it. A teacher who makes a student conform is creating unnecessary obstacles (no matter how well intentioned). More than destroying their students' chances at learning, they are in fact, destroying their own chances.

"Teaching is a heavy responsibility, so don't teach. You'll feel more relaxed."

Golden Silence

With sound,
Words lose all
Their meaning.

Three men are sitting around a table. There is a glass of water. One man says, "The glass is half empty!" The second man says, "The glass is half full!" The third man reaches over, drinks the glass and then gets up and leaves.

The Golden Hush

Silence is golden
And honest smiles move,
But who has the heart to hear
What is not being said?

A tortoise had taken up jogging. One day, a hungry wolf attacked it. Too lazy to break through the tortoise's shell, the wolf went off in search of easier prey. Buoyed by this, the tortoise thought to itself, "Can you imagine that? Who would've thought that jogging could come in so handy? Why, even a wolf is no match for me!"

Is This All?

Just words,
And nothing else.

"There are some people that if they don't know,
you can't tell them."—Louis Armstrong

Invisibility

Not much, but then,
That is the splendor
Of the teacher's art.

Isn't it interesting that one of history's most famous teachers left nothing he taught in writing? Socrates would have been proud.

※ ※ ※ ※

Modern education has a feel good sense about its methods. Students must always be satisfied. Have you ever seen cheetah cubs experimenting with a baby gazelle? Sometimes the gazelle survives.

Power

*"If you never learn to move without strength,
then you have no future in budo."*

Human beings, like many other animals, are born with the capacity to be violent. We do not need to be taught how to attack and kill. Our species would not have survived without an innate, refined killing instinct. (As with all animals) Our evolutionary niche is the refined use of power (tools and weapons).

Budo is so much more than this.

There are many kinds of power. There is the power of addiction, the power of sexual attraction, the power of an honest heart, the power of nature, the power of faith and the power of physical strength, amongst many others. The weakest of these is physical power.

Certainly, physical power can kill you. That is, in a way, the reason for budo to exist. We do not want to be immovable objects in the path of irresistible forces. We do not want to become irresistible forces ourselves. Budo is about becoming infinitely movable in the path of any and all forces.

Think about it in practical terms: How can you become strong enough, fast enough or skilful enough to keep a .45 from dropping you like a fly? You can't. Once the bullet leaves the gun, there is nothing you can do.

How much power does it take to flick an eyeball? How hard do you need to press down to cut with a razor blade? How fast do you need to be when you already know what he is going to do next?

"Use the strength of weakness."

Many people concern themselves with generating power in their punches and kicks, cutting well, penetration, and speed. Yes, one needs to learn the proper basics and the direction of such learning tends toward such descriptive terms, but the pursuit of any extreme is no longer budo. Once you have learned the skill to a perfunctory level, then you don't need to worry about it anymore. Practice the forms but don't make the mistake of becoming "result-oriented." Sensei has tried to estimate the "degree" to which we should commit at somewhere around 60% of our capacities.

You want to be able to stop at any point and change what you are doing entirely. How can you stop at any point if you believe you must complete a technique? How can you stop when you have delegated control of your mind and body to "muscle memory?" To punch someone as hard as you can or to cut completely through a target is the same as setting yourself upon a path over which you have no control.

> *"By being able to avoid injuring your partner,*
> *you can do these things that I do."*

Power is the ability to stop.

Powerful people do not require immediate gratification. Being able to defend yourself with a sword without cutting the opponent—that is power. That is control.

If there is a power to cultivate in budo, it is the heart. It takes courage to stop yourself from doing the things you want to do. A man who can resist all temptation is dangerous, indeed.

> *"Power, skill and technique are a part of the training*
> *in the beginning, but they will only take you so far.*
> *If you can't get past these ideas, however,*
> *you will not be able to float. You will sink instead."*

Secret Message

Floating bottle,
You needn't arrive
At any shore.

"You don't need any power to do this."

Catch and Release

Gone,
Never held.

Punch and Judy make no sense. Two people who live to hate each other, love to hit each other, screaming, bashing, hate each other. And they wouldn't have it any other way. Take one to paradise, make the other a king, and they'd die without that bash, bash, bash.

"Who am I?" they'd scream, "without he who makes me angry?"

"How can you know what it is to be happy without the burning pain of a stick across your back?"

"Budo is art. You cannot gain power through art.
So, some of you are wasting your time."

You have to wonder about the guy who actually does try to build a better mousetrap. Bigger springs, infrared sensors, maybe some explosives on the bar...

With a piece of broken glass in the hand, even a child can master the famous one-inch punch.

Nothing

How priceless it is,
To know the secret value.

In the story of the tortoise and the hare, the narrator never mentions how, before the race, the tortoise secretly puts sleeping powder into the hare's drinking water...

"We are studying the art of controlling without power."

The Nature of Space

Infinite spaces
Were yours to command…
What idle dreaming!
Such space as I saw
Was simply you,
Out of the way.

"I am following Nature without being able to grasp her."
—Claude Monet

The Feeling—Natural Justice in Motion

"Don't squeeze the bee."

Every single lesson by the grandmaster is a lesson on the "feeling." Every single thing he says, writes, does is an expression of this "feeling." The feeling IS budo. The techniques, the scrolls, the history the oral transmissions, everything that can be found in budo is there to pass on this lesson, the "feeling."

> *"Many think that the 'inner secrets' are the pinnacle but really, that's not true."*

Whole books could be written on this subject and still fail to convey its importance, let alone its meaning. The reason behind this is simple: the "feeling" is not something that you can know. It could be expressed, perhaps, as something that is familiar or something you recognize. Try to explain an orgasm in words to someone who has never had one. Try to explain grief. If you could, there would be no such thing as art.

It is impossible to put into words something that a person has not experienced for himself or herself. The "feeling" in budo is the same. Words are not enough to do it justice. Pictures may tell a thousand words but what if the word you really need is not there? The "feeling" is the experience of budo's expression through you.

> *"The forms and such are not important.*
> *You must study the feeling."*

If you look to what is clearly understandable, you will remove yourself from the study of the "feeling." One can find many ideas within the "feeling," some of which have been discussed in this book. On one level, it is the sensation of lightly moving to safe places so that doing things becomes unnecessary and the opponent, unable to understand what is happening, injures himself. By letting the opponent decide whether he is guilty or not, whether he suffers or not, the meaning of the martial phrase, "natural justice," becomes clear. Without the "feeling" though, any justice becomes merely human justice.

There is an old budo parable about holding a bee in your hand. If you squeeze the bee, it will sting you out of self-defense. If your hands are merely cupped around the bee, it does not know it has been captured and feels no desire to sting you.

The "feeling" involves putting into play, all of the elements touched upon so far. You are not there to beat the opponent into submission. The "feeling" does not require you to show your opponent your skill, experience, or intelligence. The "feeling" is that of you not being there. Consider it as a non-physical connection with your opponent where his intentions become clear to you. Before his intentions become movement, his world changes, just ever so slightly. He feels nothing. He gets no feedback from his attacks. He starts to react, trying to make true his thoughts and desires. In time, he becomes concerned, frightened even. You have penetrated his heart. If your opponent is sensitive enough, he will know that he has been mortally wounded.

"You are hurting him by not hurting him."

Think about that: it is almost like mind reading. Perhaps it is just a matter of the opponents' senses being dulled that yours seem heightened. Whatever the case, since you have no desire, no intentions at all, your opponent falls into a void—one of his own making. Only when he has put himself into this dire situation and only when you are safe, do you act. Your action, quite literally, is his. This is Natural Justice.

"This is training, this movement, moving with each other and following your opponent."

The "feeling" is a kind of personal intimacy that most people only experience with their loved ones. Can't you tell what your loved ones are feeling just by the "air" that surrounds them? Take that ability, remove all the sentiment, and apply it in the dojo.

Surrender control of the fight to your opponent. It takes courage to do this but if you persevere with it, you will find yourself no longer knowing where you will end up when you move, you will begin to notice that the smallest of motions as being sufficient and your opponent will have no idea what you are doing. Like a dust in the breeze, you will come to understand the value of nothingness.

"Your opponent will decide how you will move."

There is an expression in budo called, Demon Gate, or Kimon, but this expression can also be read as Life Gate. It is that place where you go, where it seems scariest, that you are safest. It requires patience to reach it though...and courage. In training, you will find yourself moving to where it is safest for you. You will have no desire to win, no desire at all to do anything other than to stay safe. It may be that the opponent will recognize that he too can stay safe. Maybe he won't. Kimon is life for whoever heads there. It is also death for those who avoid it.

"Most martial artists only know about skill and power.
That is fine but there is more. They stop at skill and
so do not know what is beyond it."

The "feeling" is not something that you do. It is not a technique that you master. It is not an emotion. It has absolutely nothing to do with martial arts. It has nothing to do with rank or how many students you have nor whether you have a dojo or not.

It has nothing to do with being a teacher. It has nothing to do with a mystical state of being. It has nothing to do with how long you have trained or how skilled you have become. If anything, these things detract from the feeling.

There are so many things that the "feeling" is not!!

The only way to get the feeling is to accept it, physically, from someone who has it. It is not a matter of hard work or desire but of acceptance. You have to feel it, recognize it and accept it. Accepting it seems to be the hardest part. Once you do, you will see it in the grandmaster and feel like someone had taken off a blindfold you had been wearing from the beginning. You will no longer need a translation. You will be "in tune."

The "feeling" makes weakness out of strength, it makes babies out of heroes and it allows you to be gentle with everyone, no matter what they intend.

*"Do not try to apply rules and logic to budo.
Budo is feeling, not form."*

If you are a fat chicken, then most branches won't hold you up for long. They start to bend down towards the ground and then they break. You can feel the branches start to shake a little when they can take no more. When they start to shake, you hop to another branch somewhere else on the tree. (Any branch is fine, it doesn't matter what it looks like, and it will be safe for a few moments at least.) The other branch thrashes around, but you are safe. That is, until this branch starts to shake.

*"The feeling is like negative one and
positive one; you are zero in between."*

*"I am teaching at the level of the skin of an egg.
You need this kind of control; that you can crack an egg
without tearing the skin underneath."*

Can you use the Ouija board? Can you let the spirits move the piece under your fingertips or do you move it yourself and pretend? Only a child would be fooled.

"Budo is not something you need to understand academically. You only need to feel it. Budo is feeling. If you are a scholar, then studying budo and gathering information is fine, but you are not a budoka."

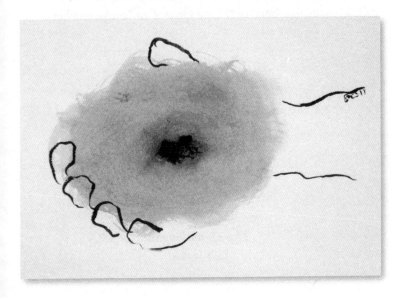

Movement

Change is eternal,
The only sign of permanence.

The trail boss wouldn't stop. He kept going past the thickets and the thorns, the rocky places and the hills, past the Indian camp and the cactus. He didn't stop until he had found a good place. Trail Boss! We have guns, we have knives, we can take care of any problem! Who made you Boss, anyway…

*"You can be very skilled at budo,
but without the feeling, you have nothing."*

Snake handlers are known for their ability to safely interact with poisonous snakes. One may note, however, that they are not called "snake grabbers" or "snake kickers" or "snake crushers."

*"I'm not doing anything.
I'm not taking anything."*

The Feeling

*Marksman,
There is nothing in
Your sights!*

There was a man who wanted to understand everything one could possibly know about butterflies. He traveled the world collecting them, taking photographs and specimens until he had every single kind of butterfly preserved in his collection. One day he was in a park, stalking a butterfly, when a child asked him a question.

"Which flower will it land on next?" asked the child.

"I have no idea," he replied.

"Does the butterfly know?"

The man could not answer. Indeed, he could not speak.

*"You can study techniques after I'm dead.
Study the feeling now."*

Isn't it odd that a girl cannot resist the softest touches, the ones she can barely feel. You might even only pretend to touch her hair. If she can't feel it at all, she will move towards it until she does. How odd, how disturbing, how natural—that killing and loving should be so similar.

I am the circle within a circle. I am the sphere within a sphere. In going nowhere, I am already there. In waiting for you to leave, I await your arrival.

The Forms of Earth and Space

*Soaring Into the sky
I know you dragon,
Your wings nothing more
Than feet firmly planted
On the ground.*

"Every movement is an expression of the feeling.
The outcome may be different each time,
and it may be seen as art,
but the underlying principle is the same."

Dream Lover

All I have ever done,
Is give you what you want.

"Budo is feeling.
If anybody says that the way to understand budo is by
studying forms, he is mistaken."

The Movement of Eternity

Do you know the source of this change?
It is a divine movement,
Taking place in the symphony of the heart.

Tales of Budo

Starting Off

Gari and Aho were long time friends.

Gari was a very friendly, clever and talkative parrot that used to love flying up to try and touch the sun. Deep down, he knew that he could never actually reach it but that shiny ball in the sky used to always tempt him to at least try.

Aho, a donkey, was friendly and clever as well and while he tried very hard to understand his friend's fascination with touching the sun, he was more interested in tending to the garden patches that lay along the river that flowed from the mountain nearby.

On one particularly fine morning, with the sun shining brightly and bathing the land in warm sunlight Gari, in his usual conversative self, convinced himself that, "THIS is the day I'll finally reach the sun. I'm going to do it!"

Committed, resolved and with his eyes on the target, Gari also convinced Aho to carry him up to the nearby mountain—Mount Impossible—from where he would be able to launch himself towards his cherished goal.

In preparation for the trip, supplies were readied and loaded onto Aho's back. Water and grains were purchased from a nearby town (a poster calling attention to the supply store had been attached to a tree close by) as well as a map to the top of the mountain.

So with all of their supplies purchased and in order, the two friends began Gari's journey to the top of Mount Impossible from where Gari would be able to finally achieve his goal of touching the sun…

The Friendly Salamander

A salamander who had once lived for a time near the summit of Mount Impossible had moved to the base of the mountain and built a house there. It was a nice house, made from some stones and soil that had been delivered from the summit. The salamander took much pleasure in maintaining his lovely home, especially the road leading to it. He especially enjoyed visits from passersby and would often say, "We're all friends, even if we've never met."

Now, at this time, the two friends, Gari and Aho, had decided to pause for a rest by the River Mirror, which was in full flow due to the snow melting from Mount Impossible's summit. The two friends had been journeying along the river and, being a bit thirsty, decided to stop and take a drink of water from their supplies. Gari, in particular, was quite parched though their water supplies were running low. "This water just has the best taste, wouldn't you agree? When we run out, we'll have to order some more, don't you think?" Aho looked at him and asked, "Why don't we just drink from the river?" With a shocked look to his face, Gari blurted out, "Drink from the river?!? Why, you would need to clean it first. We don't have time for that!"

Now, the salamander had been watching this exchange, and he smiled, thinking to himself, "Wow, friends! I can invite them to my house and offer them my water. What a nice person I am." With that, he made his way to over to Gari and Aho.

"My, I couldn't help but overhear that you were low on water. Do you know me? I live at the base of Mount Impossible. I love to help people when they need it. Can I help you in anyway? I have lots of fresh water for your journey to wherever it is you are going. Are you going somewhere?"

"Of course we have heard of you," replied Gari. "You're known for having a fine house built from stone and soil from the top of Mount Impossible. We would love to be helped by you!"

Aho silently watched as his friend left him to follow the salamander to his home.

The Two Mad Monkeys

Several days after leaving his friend, the salamander, Aho, came across a strange commotion. Ahead of him he could hear two animated and excitable voices. As he drew closer, he saw two monkeys pushing a large round vegetable up the mountain. The monkeys were small, funny-looking creatures and the vegetable was much larger than they were. Curious as to why they were pushing a large, round vegetable up a mountain path, Aho approached closer.

"Hello." he said, "How are you both this morning?" They did not respond. In fact, they did not even notice that he was there since they were very busy chattering with each other. Now, Aho had no idea what they were talking about, but since they seemed to be going in the same direction as he, he decided to travel with them (whether they noticed him or not).

"Baked sweet potato tastes like a woman," said one monkey

"What?! Baked sweet potato is red banana," replied the other.

"A red banana? What on earth does a red banana taste like?"

"I've never had a red banana, but I've had plenty of baked sweet potatoes. That's how I know!"

"Well, I've had plenty of women and I know what I'm talking about."

"But I've never seen you eat sweet potato!"

"You're not supposed to eat it, just taste it."

"If you don't eat the potato, how will you ever grow a potato inside of yourself?"

"Bah! If you save your money you can always buy some later. Don't you know anything?"

"You don't know anything!"

"Yes I do. I'm pushing a potato up this mountain."

"Are you mad? I'm pushing this potato, not you. Talking with you is pointless!"

"I told you that before we started! You never listen!"

"How can I listen if you don't stop talking? You're a chatterbox! That's what you are!"

"A chatterbox? You've just never had a woman."

"Ah, now I see the problem. You don't realize that the only way to really understand something is to eat it."

"So what am I supposed to do… eat a woman?"

"If you are serious about all this, you will have to try it at some point."

"Eating a woman? Now I know you're crazy. What about the red bananas?"

"Who's talking about red bananas? I'm talking about tasting women."

"And then what, I become a woman?"

"No. You'd become a sweet potato and that would be an improvement."

"Hmm. Well, at least we can agree that pickling a potato is

the best way to prepare it."

"Well, it's not like we have much choice. Raw potato is poisonous."

"I never heard that before. Where did you learn this?"

"I heard someone say it."

"Gotta be true, then."

"Also, potato has to be pickled for thirty years to make it soft enough to taste."

"My mother always fried it up and smothered it with honey."

"Why would she do something so stupid?"

"So she could eat it."

"But you don't?"

"Oh hell no. I put them in my ear."

"Of course you did."

"Yeah, in my tree, we all put potatoes in our ears. That's the only way to really feel a potato."

"Potato is for chewing, not touching. You pickle it for thirty years, fry it, then chew it and spit it out."

"Why?"

"Potato juice is poisonous!"

"Then why would we chew it?"

"Is there no end to your stupidity?"…

The Famous Panther

There was once a panther who was very famous among his friends who all knew how famous he was. This panther was very proud of the fact that he was so famous. He wasn't exactly sure what he was famous for but as he was a panther and since he knew panthers hunted, he knew that he must be famous for hunting. Now, he was very proud of his hunting skill because everyone knew that panthers (who were known for hunting), were always successful when they hunted. He couldn't remember the last time he had been hunting but being a panther famous for hunting, he did know that he had been successful at it.

Now, it just so happened that this panther was admiring his hunting skills when he spied a lone donkey travelling along the mountain trail. He became very excited and wondered whether a donkey would be an easy target for a hunting panther. He had heard stories about how successful panthers were in hunting donkeys and he knew that being a successful panther, that he had hunted many donkeys (they were very famous stories and he was sure that the donkey would be in awe of them). Full of confidence, the panther secretly began following the lone donkey.

After stalking the donkey all day, the panther began to notice that the donkey's hooves were quite hard and he wondered if they were dangerous. After thinking about it, he realized that the donkey must be very afraid of him (after all, he was a famous panther) and that it would be no challenge for a famous panther like himself to defeat such a frightened donkey. He had heard that it was a great thing to spare a donkey and so the panther decided to run past the poor, unsuspecting donkey and head back home.

Gathering himself, he raced back down the trail and passed the donkey in a silent blur of proud accomplishment. Aho never even knew what didn't hit him.

The Stern Koala

After a while, Aho came across a clearing. The sun was quite warm and as he was feeling a little tired, he decided to rest for a while in the shade besides the clearing. As he sat down, he saw that in the middle of the clearing stood a koala. Now, this koala appeared to be a rather stern figure as he was standing in the middle of the clearing in a fearsome pose. He also appeared to have something strapped to his head.

"Hello. You seem to be quite fearsome. If you don't mind me

asking, what is that strapped to your head?"

"Pfft. You don't know? It's a potato."

"Oh. So why do you have a potato strapped to your head?"

"Pfft. If you are trying to reach the summit of Mount Impossible, really, you ought to know that you have to be light enough to get up there."

"I see."

"Pfft. You have to wear a potato strapped to your head. Each day you add another potato, and then another, until your head is full of potatoes."

"How does that help to make you lighter?"

"Pfft. It's so obvious. It makes you lighter because once your head is full of potatoes you can then start to remove the potatoes. Once all of the potatoes are removed, your body will be light enough to reach the top of the mountain."

"I see. So, you become lighter than before you started to strap potatoes to your head?"

The Koala looked at Aho sternly.

"Pfft, you really don't get it, do you?

The Fast-Talking Puffer Fish

A puffer fish who had seen some of the water from Mount Impossible knew that many people wanted to drink that water. Now, as tasting water was very important, he decided to make a sandwich. "Yep, this sandwich tastes good man, real good and, you know, there's water in it, so yeah, how about that?" With this in mind, the puffer fish started to make sandwiches for people who would try and walk up Mount Impossible. After the first week of eating the sandwiches that he was offering, he decided that he ought to call the sandwiches "water."

"Like, yep, there's water in these sandwiches and so yeah, you know, water's where it's at. Actually, you know, I think I'll, yeah, carbonate the water, that's what I'll do. Give it a bit o' fizz for the biz. Yeah, that'll go down well."

Now it just so happened that Aho came across the puffer fish eating (drinking) his sandwiches (water).

"Hello, are you offering sandwiches to people on the way to Mount Impossible?"

"Hey! I started offering water a week ago."

"Well, water is important."

"Yep, yep. That's right. You look like you've seen water before. It's good that we see eye-to-eye, so yeah, we ought to… collaborate, yeah, and work together. If people can't get to Mount Impossible, they can have some of my water. I do my best to offer water so that they can, you know, keep up their electrolyte levels. That's why I carbonate it. Give it a bit o' fizz for the biz, you know." He offered Aho a sandwich, "Here you go man, have some water." Aho reached for the sandwich and went to take a bite before the puffer fish stopped him.

"No dude, you don't eat it man, you put it on your head."

"Excuse me?"

"Yeah man, you put it on your head and you know, you let the water, you know, the bubbles, soak into your head."

"Into your head?"

"Yeah, dude, carbonated water is really good for this. You got to, you know, top up your electrolyte levels all the time man." Aho noticed that the puffer fish's body was swelling and expanding the more he spoke.

"Please be careful, you seem to be swelling and expanding the more you speak!"

"Relax dude, I'm just offering water to help people top up, you know, my electrolyte levels. You know? Got to keep the fizz in the biz, you know." Incredibly, as his body continued to swell and get larger, the puffer fish started to rise and float away.

"Where are you going? Come back!"

"Haha, you worry too much man. Relax and drink the water. It's carbonated, you know."

The Thoughtful Rooster

There was once a rooster who enjoyed walking along the edge of a small pond by the trail. The water in the pond was very clear and the rooster would always make a point of not glancing at the reflection of himself in it. He was quite sure that this effort of his was a sign of his wisdom. Every now and then, a few people walking along the trail would stop by the pond to relax. It was at these times that he would perform for himself the selfless task of providing important information about Mount Impossible.

"In my former life, it was suggested that I was a newscaster," the rooster crowed.

The people relaxing by the pond would throw their hands in the air and cheer, "Yay! That's great!. We love hearing the news."

"I'm very good, you see, at summarizing the news." The rooster glanced at his reflection in the pond, before turning back to his audience. "And as you know, I'm well placed in being able to provide such news. In fact," glancing again at the pond, "I'm quite sure that, now that I think about it, it is like a balloon that continues to…" he opened up his wings, "…expaaaand."

"Oooh!" the people by the pond gasped, "Did you hear that? He said it was like a balloon that continues to…" everyone extended their arms out, "…expaaand."

"Yes, yes, it's true! Balloons do continue to expand," one replied.

"Oh, this is great!" said another.

The rooster glanced again at the pond's surface. He fluffed up his tail-feathers and turned back to his audience.

"Coming up with the…appropriate…descriptions that best describe the news is difficult and I do try my best because…" he paused, "…as you all know, the news is like a corkscrew that continues to…" his nostrils flared, "…unwiiiind."

"Yay!" the audience cheered, "Wow! Corkscrews really do unwind!" As one, the audience cried out, "Your descriptions are great!" One member of the audience was so excited he got up from his seat and presented the rooster with a t-shirt. Unfurling it, the rooster saw that his face was printed on it. He smiled and thanked the audience member for the kind gift.

The rooster stood for a moment, proud of the fact that everyone said the same thing to him at the same time. He also knew that because people listened to him, that he must be wise. This thought made him feel giddy with maturity. Glancing once more into the pond, the rooster put on the t-shirt, fluffed up his tail-feathers once more and turned back to his audience.

The Leaping Pony

Aho rounded a bend in the trail and came across a flustering display of dust and noise.

Ahead of him there was a tiny pony, leaping and jumping around, performing acrobatic tricks, all the while crying out gleefully, "Oh, how great it is to be wild and free! How great it is to be wild and free!"

Aho had never seen such behavior before and was somewhat envious. "Wow, you seem to be so happy and full of joy."

"Yes, yes, oh, how great it is to be wild and free!"

"You seem so good at leaping and jumping around. You must practice every day."

"Yes, yes, oh, how great it is to be wild and free!"

"I guess it must be great to be so wild and free," replied Aho.

"Yes, yes, oh, how great it is to be wild and free!"

By this stage, Aho started to wonder about the pony. He then noticed that the pony had blinkers on with the words "Hello, I'm a pony" engraved on them.

"May I ask your name?"

"Yes, yes, oh, how great it is to be wild and free!"

Aho wondered what was wrong with the pony. He kept saying the same thing, over and over again.

"Do you know that you keep saying the same thing, over and over again?"

"Yes, yes…"

"So why do you…"

"…oh, how great it is to be wild and free!"

Aho frowned and sat down confused. What a strange pony, he thought. He seemed to leap around so beautifully and yet he kept saying the same words over and over again. After a while of watching the pony's performance, Aho discovered that he was doing the same jumps, the same leaps, in the same order all the time. After a few more moments, Aho started to get tired of this performance and decided to continue on his way.

"Well, it was interesting meeting you. Good luck."

As Aho left him, in the background, he could hear, "Yes, yes, oh, how great it is to be wild and free!"

The Angry Goat

"Are you mad?!?"

Aho had never heard a goat react so angrily to a simple question. "I'm sorry. I just thought that if you were heading to the summit of Mount Impossible, that you would be following the trail to the top"

"Oh, for heaven's sakes man! You think you're a guide or something? That's just typical of people like you." At that, the goat started to ram his head into a rock.

CRASH! BANG!

"Well, like I said, I'm sorry if I caused you any problems."

Looking up from his rock ramming, the goat cried, "Cause me any problems? Oh, how patronizing you are. Are you always so insensitive?" He then continued on with ramming the rock.

CRASH! BANG!

"Well… like I said, I am sorry. Perhaps I should be on my way now."

The goat paused again and replied, "You think you are something special now, don't you? Well, not everyone is interested in walking up a mountain trail. I'm going through the trail. That way, I'll be able to see the whole mountain. From within!" With that, he went back to his rock ramming with a renewed vigor.

CRASH! BANG!

At that moment, Aho wondered about the goat's head. Plucking up his courage (after all, the goat was very grumpy), Aho asked, "Doesn't it hurt to ram your head into a rock so many times?"

CRASH! BANG!

"Oh… grr… now you are really making me mad! That's it! Nothing's gonna stop me now! I'm really gonna ram this rock even harder!"

CRASH! BANG!

The Peak

When Aho reached the peak, and it took far less time than he feared, he was surprised to find that there were many other creatures waiting for him, including a tiny-headed squirrel, a mouse with a moustache, and a frog with an onion in its ear.

In the middle of the clearing at the top of the mountain, there was a large stone. On the side of the stone, written with bold strokes of black, it said, "Fly." Aho went directly to the stone and perched atop it. This caught the attention of the other animals and they gathered around Aho with unfriendly faces.

"So, you think you understand, huh?" said one.

"You don't need to be up there, little donkey. It's best not to even look at this stone until you are an old man," said another.

"If you want to sit there, you might want to buy one of my birdhouses. They are not far from the stone and you can sleep there when you get tired."

"What is this place? Who left this message? What does all of this mean?" asked Aho.

No one answered. "What does "fly" mean?" he asked again.

"It doesn't mean anything, it's just a joke. I have a much smaller stone that you can sit on if you come back later." said the mouse with a moustache.

"Oh it has a meaning, it is all written down in the Secret Squirrel Scrolls," said the tiny-headed squirrel.

"You'll understand what it means after you put an onion in your ear and climb the rock ten times a day," said the frog with the onion in its ear.

Aho thought for a minute, the many voices around him blurring into one loud noise of confusion.

"What if I just did what the rock says to do? What would be wrong with that?"

The crowd around him roared in disagreement. None of them agreed with each other, though all of them disagreed with Aho's suggestion. He began to flutter off the rock, higher and higher. The crowd below screamed and wailed.

"What are you doing!?!"

"You can't fly! You don't speak the language of the rock!"

"You must carry the rock on your back; it will take years to develop such powerful wings!"

"That is not flying! Flying means walking around and flapping your wings in a manner reminiscent of flight."

Aho looked back down at the wailing crowd once, turned back towards the sky, and kept soaring higher and higher.

"You can only go so far in the dojo with technique.
After that, you either fly or you go no further,
no matter how many years you keep training."

A Final Word

"You need a strong heart to be able to do this."

Is it cowardice or wisdom that compels us to wear our seatbelts? Seatbelts don't make you more powerful, they are not designed for that. When you think about the martial arts, you ought to think of it in the same way as a seatbelt. Budo is not a tool for ensuring your survival when you intentionally taking life-threatening risks. If anything, it is a kind of wisdom that reminds us of the value of staying alive.

Much has been made of the ninja as scouts and spies. Like a military scout or even modern day elite military units, the ninja were known for their skills in escape, evasion, and secret observation. Their job was not to engage the enemy but to gather information, in person, and that meant staying out of sight and avoiding conflict at all costs.

But that was at one point in history.

What of the rest of their history? Consider the saying, "There is a time for peace and a time for war." Did the ninja whom we never hear about understand this? General Macarthur once said something along the lines of, "Old soldiers never die, they just fade away." Perhaps it is just as well that the ninja, and others around the world who discovered and lived through violence, did just that.

For us today, the lessons about the value of life, its fragility, and the vulnerability of all people, ought to be clear. The ninja, and those like them, survived, adapting to the times to ensure their continuing presence. The wisdom behind this seems clear but human history is replete with those who failed to live long enough to see it.

It takes tremendous faith to accept budo and to be changed by it. The level of courage it takes to throw away the world of forms and become zero is great and respect is due to any person who can do it. Understandably, very few people can.

There is no real final word in budo. It just keeps going, like it has always done and always will. But if there is one thing that we would like the reader to know, it is this: it takes a simple kind of honest courage to follow a master. Sometimes you stumble and your course changes but that honest courage will always bring you back.

To have faith in something that will change your soul is a lonely endeavor but others have done it, and survived. Others will continue to do it.

They too will survive.

Again

Here we are again,
And again.

Acknowledgments

There have been many people we have encountered in our studies who have made an impact upon us: Duncan Stewart, Ed Lomax, Darren Horvarth, Mark Lithgow, Mike Loonam, Paul Masse, Doug Wilson, Kenji Mukai,. Yet none of them, despite our respect for them, can compare in influence to Masaaki Hatsumi, or as we usually call him, Sensei.

Many years ago we stumbled upon a martial arts master and it is only now that the wounds from that encounter have begun healing.

Thank you Sensei.

Dragon Flight

Over there,
In the nether land,
Your wings rest,
In flight.

Patience, Providence, Acceptance.

The Tuttle Story: "Books to Span the East and West"

Most people are surprised to learn that the world's largest publisher of books on Asia had its humble beginnings in the tiny American state of Vermont. The company's founder, Charles Tuttle, came from a New England family steeped in publishing, and his first love was books—especially old and rare editions.

Tuttle's father was a noted antiquarian dealer in Rutland, Vermont. Young Charles honed his knowledge of the trade working in the family bookstore, and later in the rare books section of Columbia University Library. His passion for beautiful books—old and new—never wavered through his long career as a bookseller and publisher.

After graduating from Harvard, Tuttle enlisted in the military and in 1945 was sent to Tokyo to work on General Douglas MacArthur's staff. He was tasked with helping to revive the Japanese publishing industry, which had been utterly devastated by the war. When his tour of duty was completed, he left the military, married a talented and beautiful singer, Reiko Chiba, and in 1948 began several successful business ventures.

To his astonishment, Tuttle discovered that postwar Tokyo was actually a book-lover's paradise. He befriended dealers in the Kanda district and began supplying rare Japanese editions to American libraries. He also imported American books to sell to the thousands of GIs stationed in Japan. By 1949, Tuttle's business was thriving, and he opened Tokyo's very first English-language bookstore in the Takashimaya Department Store in Ginza, to great success. Two years later, he began publishing books to fulfill the growing interest of foreigners in all things Asian.

Though a westerner, Tuttle was hugely instrumental in bringing a knowledge of Japan and Asia to a world hungry for information about the East. By the time of his death in 1993, he had published over 6,000 books on Asian culture, history and art—a legacy honored by Emperor Hirohito in 1983 with the "Order of the Sacred Treasure," the highest honor Japan bestows upon non-Japanese.

The Tuttle company today maintains an active backlist of some 1,500 titles, many of which have been continuously in print since the 1950s and 1960s—a great testament to Charles Tuttle's skill as a publisher. More than 60 years after its founding, Tuttle Publishing is more active today than at any time in its history, still inspired by Charles Tuttle's core mission—to publish fine books to span the East and West and provide a greater understanding of each.